The Religious Sense

The Religious Sense, the fruit of many years of dialogue with students, is an exploration of the search for meaning in life. Luigi Giussani shows that the nature of reason expresses itself in the ultimate need for truth, goodness, and beauty. These needs constitute the fabric of the religious sense, which is evident in every human being everywhere and in all times. So strong is this sense that it leads one to desire that the answer to life's mystery might reveal itself in some way.

Giussani challenges us to penetrate the deepest levels of experience to discover our essential selves, breaking through the layers of opinions and judgments that have obscured our true needs. Asserting that all the tools necessary for self-discovery are inherent within us, he focuses primarily on reason, not as narrowly defined by modern philosophers, but as an openness to existence, a capacity to comprehend and affirm reality in all of its dimensions.

Part of the so-called new religious revival, *The Religious Sense* avoids any sentimental or irrational reduction of the religious experience. It is a forthright and refreshing call to reassess our lives.

MONSIGNOR LUIGI GIUSSANI has written more than twenty books. In 1995 he was awarded Italy's prestigious National Catholic Culture Prize.

The Religious Sense

LUIGI GIUSSANI

Translated by John Zucchi

McGill-Queen's University Press
Montreal & Kingston • London • Buffalo

© McGill-Queen's University Press 1997
ISBN 0-7735-1626-3

Legal deposit fourth quarter 1997
Bibliothèque nationale du Québec

Printed in Canada on acid-free paper
Reprinted in paper 1998

McGill-Queen's University Press acknowledges the
support of the the Canada Council for the Arts
for its publishing program.

Permissions for quoted texts appear on 165–6.

Canadian Cataloguing in Publication Data

Giussani, Luigi, 1922–
    The religious sense
    Translation of: Il senso religioso.
    Includes bibliographical references.
    ISBN 0-7735-1626-3
    1. Religion. 2. Reason. 3. Life. I. Zucchi, John E.,
    1955– II. Title
    BL48.G5813 1997   200   C97-900317-2

This is a completely revised version of a
translation published in 1990 by Ignatius Press.

Cover: *Treppe und Leiter (Stairs and Ladder)* 1928,
183 (J3) by Paul Klee
14.5 x 14.5 cm.
Oil on plaster-primed canvas
Musée National d'Art Moderne, Paris
© 1997 Artists Rights Society (ARS), New York/
VG Bild-Kunst, Bonn.

Contents

Foreword

In this beautifully crafted work, Luigi Giussani draws us into a world of beauty and power by bringing us closer to life in all its shimmering intensity. We lose this world in an age of ideology as we manipulate, fabricate, and strive to master reality. We overvalue our own schemes. We forget that there is a world we are invited to know – to know and, yes, to love. The religious experience, for Giussani, is all about reality, especially that reality we call "human" which cannot be "studied as a geological or meteorological event." Why? Because it "involves the person." The person is one who engages, seeks, works, yearns, loves. We come to know the world and others precisely because we are drawn out of ourselves and toward an object outside ourselves. We move toward a reality we did not make. Abstract, logical processes take us only so far. If carried to an extreme, systems of thought lose a connection to reality and become self-confirming. We live in the rarified realm of pure thought. We deny that some things are evident and that they make themselves known to us: there is a presence "one must admit." Giussani challenges us to love "the truth of an object more than your own attachment to the opinions you have already formed about it. More concisely, one could say, 'love the truth more than yourself.' "

This is a very unfashionable way of talking as we near the end of the twentieth century. We believe that we are sovereign in all things. We hold no truths as self-evident. Truth, we are told, is nothing but the arbitrary imposition on human subjects of the partial views of the more powerful. We live in a cynical time. Yet, here is this man, Giussani, calling us to wonder and to awe. It is the religious sense – a "radical engagement of the self with life" – that alone enables us to fulfil the promise of the scripture that we might have life and might have it more abundantly. How sad it is that our quest for self-mastery and a widespread sense of emptiness and loss-of-meaning go hand-in-hand, yet we often fail to see the connection. Giussani helps us to fit the broken pieces together by refusing seductive schemes and manipulations, including a quest for perfection that can only end in ashes and misery. He holds up to the light the infinite worth of the human person and, as he does so, he helps us to realize that it is in the light of the ultimate that the penultimate takes form. In an era that ill-dignifies human beings in so many ways, Giussani reminds us that human dignity is not for sale.

Jean Bethke Elshtain
Laura Spelman Rockefeller Chair
of Social and Political Ethics
University of Chicago

Introduction

With this present volume, *The Religious Sense*, McGill-Queen's University Press begins the publication of the fundamental works of Monsignor Luigi Giussani. To be published in three volumes, the text makes available in English the content of the courses presented by Monsignor Giussani in over forty years of teaching, first as a teacher of religion in a Milan high school, and later, beginning in 1964, as professor of Introduction to Theology at the Catholic University of the same city. Following this first volume, the next will be dedicated to the great personal self-revelation of God in the world in the person of Jesus Christ (*At the Origin of the Christian Claim*), while the third and final text shall treat the way in which this event remains present in the church for all time and in every age (*Why the Church?*).

In Monsignor Giussani's work, what we discover is not simply a theological treatise in the technical sense, born from elaborated theory. Instead, we encounter a series of reflections which, while taking nothing away from the rigor and systematisation of thought, are born from Monsignor Giussani's educational preoccupation to communicate the reasonableness of the "Christian fact" precisely through one's experience of his or her own humanity.

One can better understand the originality of the method and the content of these three volumes (which are found at the centre of extensive works that include more than twenty major reflections and many articles) when one recalls that the person of Monsignor Giussani is at the origin of one of the most active and engaged movements in the church and society today, Communion and Liberation. Present already in more than seventy countries ("Go out to all the world ..."

was the mandate Pope John Paul II gave to the movement on the occasion of the thirtieth anniversary of its founding), its adult section, the "Fraternity of Communion and Liberation," has been recognised by the Holy See as a universal association of the Christian faithful of pontifical right. For all of these reasons, I am pleased and honoured, as the recently-appointed president of the Pontifical Council for the Laity, to introduce these texts.

Communion and Liberation has its roots in the 1960s when Monsignor Giussani, then a young member of the Faculty of Theology of Milan, engaged in intense study of the thought of American Protestantism, especially that of Reinhold Neibuhr. At that time, he decided to forgo specialised theological teaching in order to dedicate himself to being completely present to the students. In a society such as Italy's in the 1960s, at least still in appearance profoundly permeated by the principles of Catholicism, Monsignor Giussani understood with dramatic clarity the risks of slipping into merely formal adhesion to these same principles, especially on the part of the young. Furthermore, he intuited with much anticipation succeeding developments in society and the church – the drama of a reduction of the Christian fact to merely practical and exterior practice, implying for Christians the loss of real consciousness of the faith's foundations and of its implications for all of human existence. Ultimately, therefore, without a foundation of reason, faith would be based simply upon sentimentality; it would no longer be of concern to the human person; it would be without influence on reality; and thus de facto faith would become subordinated to whatever dominant values prevailed in the current social mentality.

From his very first experiences as a teacher, Monsignor Giussani sought passionately to affirm the clarity and to illuminate in all of its aspects the reasonableness of Christianity. Even recently in an article which appeared in an Italian daily on the occasion of Christmas, 1996, Monsignor Giussani affirmed his fundamental educational concern. "The first problem which we encounter in regard to modern culture is that we are beggars before the concept of reason. It is as if no one any longer possesses the concept of reason. Yet we understand, to the contrary, that faith requires that the human person use reason in order that he might recognise the gracious event of God among us."

According to the author, modern mentality reduces reason to a series of categories into which reality is forced to enter. What cannot be forced into these categories is defined as irrational. But reason, instead, is opened wide to reality, it takes it all in, noting its connections and its implications. Reason discourses about reality, seeks to get inside its perceived meaning, moving from one angle to the next, storing everything in its memory and tending to embrace it all. Reason is that which defines us as human persons. For this, it is necessary to have a true passion for reasonableness.

In his first volume, the author explains the notion that the very essence of rationality and the roots of human conscience are found in the religious sense of the individual. Christianity speaks to this religious sense precisely because it presents itself as an unforeseen possibility (who could have predicted the death and Resurrection of the only Son of God?) to the desire of the human person to live in such a way as to seek, discover, and then love his true destiny. Christianity, therefore, shows itself to be a reasonable response to the deepest desire of humanity. Indeed, every human being by the simple fact that he exists affirms in his existence, if even unconsciously, the absolute reason why it is worth the trouble of living. In this way, it appears as a requirement of reason to know both the scope of the existing reality and of history, namely, to know that which has always been referred to as "Mystery," or God. In every act of reason, following every possible step of identifiable logic, there comes a point, an opening, an inspiration, an unforeseen insight through which every experience that might be judged by reason can only be judged in the light of the unique reality of Mystery, of God. If reason is faithful to its original dynamism of openness to the totality of reality, it recognises the existence of this ultimate, mysterious level of reality. But it cannot pretend with its own forces to know "Who" the Mystery may be.

Mystery makes himself known only when he reveals himself, taking the initiative to place himself as a factor in human experience when and as he wills. Reason, in fact, anticipates this "revelation," but it cannot make it happen. And yet, to deny the possibility of this initiative on the part of Mystery, as happens in large measure in much of modern culture, is ultimately to deny reason as a category of the possibility of a relationship with the Infinite, of a relationship with the being that is Mystery.

At a certain historical moment one man, Jesus of Nazareth, not only revealed the mystery of God but identified himself with it. How this event began to draw the attention of men; how Jesus brought about a clear conviction in those who began to follow him; in what way he communicated the mystery of his person; how he confirmed his self-revelation with a new and perfect understanding of human life – all of this constitutes the content of the second volume of the series, *At the Origin of the Christian Claim*.

Yet today, after 2000 years, how is it possible to be certain concerning the fact of Christ? How is it reasonable today to adhere to the

Christian claim? This problem identifies the heart of what has histori-cally been called "the church," that socially identifiable phenomenon that presents itself in history as the continuation of the event of Christ. Today, as 2000 years ago, the only way to know Christ certain-ly is through an encounter with the human reality in which he is present. Thus, the entire treatise with which the author deals in the third volume, *Why the Church?* can be summed up in this: the church presents itself as a human phenomenon which claims to carry within itself the divine. As such, the presence of the church in the history of humanity continually confronts the world in the same way as Christ.

The work of Monsignor Giussani represents a significant contribu-tion for all those who, whether inside or outside of the church, desire to draw nearer to it without prejudgments and with a real openness to the wonderful possibilities that the coming of Christ represents. How wonderful are the possibilities even today in a time, as the author observes, "when what is called Christianity seems to be both known and yet forgotten. Known, because many are its imprints in history and in the education of peoples. And yet forgotten, because the content of its message seems to speak with difficulty to the life of the vast majority of people."

With an immediate freshness born of an intense existential experience and with surprising intensity of reflection, every passage of this work proposes in a concise and fascinating way the originality of the Christian event, of God with us, who has chosen to encounter man by becoming man, communicating himself to the world and to men and women of every time and place.

Monsignor J. Francis Stafford
President
Pontifical Council for the Laity

Preface

This trilogy makes no other claim than to affirm the truth. Its aim is to indicate how the Christian problem arose, even historically. Although the sequence of chapters does not pretend to deal exhaustively with all the problems it does indicate the path to be followed: the path of reasonableness. God, in fact, revealing himself in time and space, responds to a human need.

Today it is frequently said that reason has nothing to do with faith. But what is faith? What is reason?

Modern mentality reduces reason to a group of categories in which reality is forced to find a place, and whatever does not fall into these categories is defined as irrational. But reason is like an eye staring at reality, greedily taking it in, recording its connections and implications, penetrating reality, moving from one thing to another yet conserving all of them in memory, trying to embrace everything. A human being faces reality using reason. *Reason is what makes us human.* Therefore, we must have a passion for reasonableness, and this passion is the thread that will lead us through this discussion. For just this reason, the first volume of the Trilogy, *The Religious Sense,* opens with a threefold methodological premise to help us to grasp the way the human conscience, by nature, reasons.

Spring 1997

The Religious Sense

1 The First Premise: Realism

In order to examine the theme of the religious sense in a clear and, therefore, more efficacious manner, I shall base the method of this work on three premises. To introduce the first of these, I shall quote a passage from Alexis Carrel's *Reflections on Life:*

In the soothing softness of the modern world, the mass of traditional rules which gave consistency to life broke up as the frozen surface of a stream breaks up in spring ... Thanks to the progress of technology, the greater part of the restraints imposed on us by the cosmos have disappeared and, along with them, the creative personal effort which those restraints demanded ... The frontiers of good and evil have vanished in a mist of ideologies, whims, and appetites ... As everyone knows, few observations and much discussion are conducive to error: much observation and little discussion to truth.[1]

I would like to interrupt here to note that in this passage Carrel uses the language of one who has always dedicated himself to the study of science (let us recall that he was a young Nobelist in medicine): the word "discussion" could effectively be replaced with the phrase "argument in the service of an ideology." In fact, ours – continues Carrel – is an age of ideologies, in which, instead of learning from reality in all its aspects and building on it, man seeks to manipulate reality according to coherent schemes fabricated by the intellect; "thus the triumph of ideologies ratifies the defeat of civilization."[2]

THE METHOD OF RESEARCH IS IMPOSED BY
THE OBJECT: A REFLECTION ON ONE'S OWN
EXPERIENCE

Carrel's passage has introduced aptly the title of the first premise: for a serious inquiry into any event or "thing," we need *realism*.

By realism I refer to the urgent necessity not to give a more important role to a scheme already in our minds, but rather to cultivate an entire, passionate, insistent ability to observe the real event, the fact. Saint Augustine, with a cautious play on words, affirms something similar with this declaration: "I inquire in order to know something, not to think it."[3] Such an assertion is indicative of an attitude opposed to the one more frequently found in modern man, whereby it is held that, in fact, if we know something, we can also say that we think it. Saint Augustine, however, warns us that the contrary is not true. To think something is an intellectual, ideal and imaginative activity regarding the object and often, in giving too much weight to thought, without even realizing it – or, in reality, even justifying it – we project what we think onto the fact. The sane man, instead, wants to know about the fact, to know what it is, and only then can he also think it.

Carrel's and Saint Augustine's observations lead me to insist on emphasizing that, for the religious experience, it is important, primarily, to know what it is, what exactly we are dealing with. It is clear, in any case, that, above all, we are dealing with a fact, from a statistical standpoint the most widespread aspect of human activity. Indeed, no human activity is more extensive than what we call "religious experience or sentiments." It proposes to man a question regarding everything he does, and thus becomes a much broader point of view than any other. The question of religious awareness, of the religious sense – as we shall see – is: "What is the meaning of everything?" We must understand that, when discussing this religious sense, we are dealing with something that has been an integral aspect of man's behaviour in all times and tends to affect all human activity.

Thus, because we wish to know what this fact is, of what this religious sense consists, the problem of method concerns us immediately and acutely. How shall we face this phenomenon to ensure that we will succeed in knowing it well?

We must note here that most people, when it comes to this, either consciously or unconsciously, trust the words of others, especially those with prestigious or influential positions – philosophers whom we have studied in school or journalists who write in the newspapers or magazines that determine and form public opinion. Shall we turn to these individuals to discover what this religious sense is? Shall we study what Aristotle, Plato, Kant, Marx, or Engels say about it? We could do this, but, as a first step, the method would be incorrect. When we deal with this fundamental expression of man's existence, we simply cannot abandon ourselves to the opinions of others, absorbing the most fashionable views or impressions that determine our milieu.

Realism requires a certain method for observing and coming to know an object, and this method must not be imagined, thought of or organized and created by the subject: it must be imposed *by the object*. Perhaps a brief example will illustrate my point. Suppose I were to find myself before an audience with my notebook on a table and, if while speaking, I were to notice it out of the corner of my eye and were to wonder what that white object might be. I could think of many possibilities: ice cream spread out over the table, or even a rag. But the method for knowing what it truly is, is imposed by the object itself; I cannot contemplate a red object at the back of the room or a person's eyes in the front row in order to know the white object. If I truly wish to know it, I have no choice but to look down and fix my eyes on the object itself.

This means that the method of knowing an object is dictated by the object itself and cannot be defined by me. If, in the place of the notebook, we supposed that our eyes could perceive the religious experience as a phenomenon, even in this case, we would have to say that the method for knowing it must be suggested by the religious experience itself.

What type of phenomenon is the religious experience? It is a phenomenon that concerns human reality and therefore cannot be studied as a geological or meteorological event. It involves the person. How then must we conduct our inquiry? Since we are dealing with something that occurs within me, that has to do with my conscience, my "I" as a person, it is *on myself* that I must reflect; I must inquire into myself, engage in *an existential inquiry*.

Once I have undertaken this existential investigation, I can usefully compare my results with the views of thinkers and philosophers on this matter. At this point, my self-examination will be enriched by such a comparison, and I will have avoided raising another person's opinion to the level of definition. If I did not begin with this existential inquiry, it would be like asking someone else to define a phenomenon that I experience. This external consultation must confirm, enrich, or contest the fruits of my own personal reflection. Otherwise, I would be substituting the opinion of others for a task that belongs to me, and, in the end, I would form an inevitably alienating opinion.

I would be uncritically adopting from others a conception regarding a problem important for my life and my destiny.

EXPERIENCE IMPLIES AN EVALUATION

Up to this point, we have examined only the initial stages of the procedure. After conducting an existential inquiry, we must know how to judge the results of this self-examination. Even if we avoid being alienated by what others say, we are still not exempt from the necessity of judging what we have discovered about ourselves during the course of our inquiry. In fact, without the capacity for evaluating, man cannot have any *experience at all*.

I would like to specify that the word "experience" does not mean exclusively "to try": the man of experience is not one who has accumulated "experiences" – facts and sensations – and has lumped them all together. Such an indiscriminate accumulation often destroys and empties the personality. Experience certainly means "trying" something, but primarily it also coincides with a judgment we make about what we try. As I have stated elsewhere: "Above all, the person is self-awareness. Thus, what characterizes experience is not so much action, that is, mechanically establishing relations with reality: what defines experience is *understanding* something, discovering its meaning. Thus experience implies understanding the meaning of things."[4] A judgment requires a *criterion* on the basis of which the judgment can be made. Even regarding the religious experience, we must ask, after having carried out the inquiry: what criterion should we adopt to judge what we have discovered in the course of our self-reflection?

CRITERION FOR THE EVALUATION

And so, let us ask ourselves: Where do we find the criterion that permits us to judge what we see happening in ourselves?

There are two possibilities: either the criterion on which we base our judgment of ourselves is borrowed from the outside, or it is to be found within ourselves.

If we pursue the first possibility, we shall slip into the alienating situation described earlier. Even if we had undertaken an existential inquiry, and, therefore, refused to turn to investigations carried out by others, the result would still be alienating if we drew from others the criteria for judging ourselves. Our meaning would still depend on something outside of ourselves.

At this point, you could object intelligently that since man did not exist before he came into this world, it is not possible that he can, by himself, provide a criterion for a judgment. In any case, this criterion is "given." Now, to state that this criterion is inherent within us is not to argue that we alone provide it. Rather, it is to assert that it is drawn from our nature, it is given to us as part of our very nature (where the word nature evidently implies the word God, a clue to the ultimate origins of our "I").

Only this then can be considered a reasonable, nonalienating alternative method. In conclusion, the criterion for judging this reflection on our own humanity must emerge from within the inherent structure of the human being, the structure at the origin of the person.

ELEMENTARY EXPERIENCE

All of the experiences of my humanity and of my personality are filtered through the sieve of a primordial "original experience" that constitutes my identity in the way I face everything. Each man has a right and a duty to learn that it is always possible to compare every proposal with this "elementary experience." It must also become his habit.

What constitutes this original, elementary experience? It can be described as a complex of needs and "evidences" which accompany us as we come face to face with all that exists. Nature thrusts man into a universal comparison with himself, with others, with things, and furnishes him with a complex of original needs and "evidences" which are tools for that encounter. So original are these needs or these "evidences" that everything man does or says depends on them.

These needs can be given many names. They can be summarized with different expressions (for example, the need for happiness, the need for truth, for justice, etc.). They are like a spark igniting the human motor. Prior to them, there is no movement or human dynamism. Any personal affirmation, from the most banal and ordinary to the most reflected upon and rich in consequences, can be based solely on this nucleus of original needs.

Now to define "evidences" I will return to the example of the notebook. If someone were to approach you and ask, "Are you sure that is a notebook? And if it isn't?", we would be shocked, as if we were dealing with an eccentric. Aristotle used to remark acutely that it is foolish to seek the reason for what evidence shows to be a fact.[5] No one could live sanely at the level of these absurd questions. Hence this type of evidence is also part of what I have called elementary experience.

I would like to propose another example, ludicrous but also significant. In a high school, a philosophy teacher explains: "We all have evidence that this notebook is an object outside of ourselves. There is no one who can avoid recognizing that his first impression of this notebook is that it is an object outside of himself. Let us suppose, however, that I do not know this object: it is then as if it did not exist. Knowledge, man's spirit, and energy all create this object – so much so that if man did not know it, it would be as if it did not exist." We could describe this teacher as an "idealist." Let us imagine that our teacher falls gravely ill and is replaced by another. Upon learning from the students about their regular program, the substitute teacher decides to take up the example of the permanent teacher: "We all agree that the first evidence is that this object is outside ourselves. And if it weren't? Prove to me irrefutably that it exists as an object outside ourselves." Here we have a teacher who is a sceptic or a sophist. Let us suppose that for some unforeseen reason, a third teacher enters the scene and continues on from this point. He says, "We all have the impression that this is an object outside ourselves. This evidence is primary, original. But if I do not know it? It is as if it did not exist. You see, therefore, that knowledge is the encounter between human energy and a presence. It is an event where the energy of human knowledge is assimilated to the object. How do you produce such an assimilation? This is a fascinating question that we can only partially answer. We are certain, however, that knowledge is composed of two factors." This teacher is a "realist."

NO CONOSCENZA MA COSCIENZA

We have seen three different interpretations of the same problem. Which of the three is "right?" Each is attractive and expresses a true point of view. What method do we use to decide among them? First, we shall have to examine the three opinions and measure them with the criterion of what I have called elementary experience: with those things that are immanent in our nature, the complex of needs and "evidences" that our mother gave us at birth. We must then ask ourselves: "Of the three teachers, which one uses a method that most closely corresponds to this original experience?" We shall soon discover that the third assumed a more reasonable position because he considered all of the factors involved, whereas the other teachers used a reductionist criterion.

IT IS NOT CORRECT

I proposed this example to insist on the necessity of putting this self-reflection to the test in order to come to a judgment. This test consists of a comparison between the content of the reflection itself and the original criterion. An Eskimo mother, a mother from Tierra del Fuego, and a Japanese mother all give birth to human beings, recognizable as such both by their exterior aspects and their *interior stamp*. Thus, when they will say "I," they will use this expression to refer to a multiplicity of elements derived from diverse histories, traditions, and circumstances; but undoubtedly when they say "I" they

will also use this term to indicate an inner countenance, a "heart," as
the Bible would say, which is the same in each of them, even if translated in the most diverse ways.

I identify this *heart* with what I have called elementary experience;
that is, it is something that tends to indicate totally the original
impetus with which the human being reaches out to reality, seeking
to become one with it. He does this by fulfilling a project that dictates
to reality itself the ideal image that stimulates him from within.

MAN, THE ULTIMATE JUDGE?

We have said that the criterion for judging our own relation to
ourselves, to others, to things, and to destiny is totally immanent,
inherent within our original structure. But in human society, if there
are millions of individuals who compare themselves to the world and
destiny, how is it possible to avoid subjectivizing everything to the
point where the individual would have all the power to determine his
ultimate meaning as well as any action directed toward it? Would this
not be an exaltation of anarchy, understood as an idealization of man
as the ultimate judge?

In fact, I maintain that, like pantheism, from a cosmological point
of view, anarchy from an anthropological perspective constitutes one
of the great and fascinating temptations of human thought. As I see
it, only two types of men capture entirely the grandeur of the human
being: the anarchist and the authentically religious man. By nature,
man is relation to the infinite: on the one hand, the anarchist affirms
himself to an infinite degree, while, on the other, the authentically
religious man accepts the infinite as his meaning.

I personally understood this clearly many years ago when a young
man, urged on by his mother, came to me for confession. He really
had no faith. We began to have a discussion and, at a certain point, in
the face of my diatribe, he laughed and said: "Listen, all that you are
trying so forcefully to tell me is not worth as much as what I am about
to tell you. You cannot deny that the true grandeur of man is represented by Dante's Capaneus, that giant chained by God to Hell, yet
who cries to God, 'I cannot free myself from these chains because you
bind me here. You cannot, however, prevent me from blaspheming
you, and so I blaspheme you.'[6] This is the true grandeur of man."
After being unsettled for a few seconds, I said calmly, "But isn't it
even greater to love the infinite?" The young man left. After four
months, he returned to say that for two weeks he had been receiving
the sacraments because he had been "eaten away" all summer long by
my response. He died soon after in an automobile accident.

Anarchy is the most fascinating temptation, but it is as deceitful as it is attractive. The strength of its deceit lies precisely in its appeal, which makes us forget that man is made – that at one point he does not exist and then he dies. Only pure violence can make him say, "I affirm myself against all and everything." It is much greater and truer to love the infinite, that is, to embrace reality and being rather than to assert oneself against them. Indeed, we must recognize that man truly affirms himself only by accepting reality, so much so that, in fact, he begins to accept himself by accepting his existence, that is, a reality he has not given himself.

That is why the fundamental criterion for facing things is an objective one, with which nature thrusts man into a universal comparison, endowing him with that nucleus of original needs, with that elementary experience which mothers in the *same* way provide to their children. It is only here, by affirming this common identity, that we overcome anarchy. The need for goodness, justice, truth, and happiness constitutes man's ultimate identity, the profound energy with which men in all ages and of all races approach everything, enabling them to an exchange, of not only things, but also ideas, and transmit riches to each other over the distance of centuries. We are stirred as we read passages written thousands of years ago by ancient poets, and we sense that their works apply to the present in a way that our day-to-day relations do not. If there is an experience of human maturity, it is precisely this possibility of placing ourselves in the past, of approaching the past as if it were near, a part of ourselves. Why is this possible? Because this elementary experience, as we stated, is substantially the same in everyone, even if it will then be determined, translated, and realized in very different ways – so different, in fact, that they may seem opposed.

ASCESIS FOR LIBERATION

I would, therefore, say: if we wish to become adults without being cheated, alienated, enslaved by others, or exploited, we must become accustomed to comparing everything with this elementary experience. In reality, then, I propose a task that is neither easy nor popular. Normally, everything is approached from the perspective of the common mentality which, in turn, is publicized and sustained by whomever holds the reins of power in society. Consequently, family tradition or the tradition of the broader society in which we have grown up, obscures or hardens over our original needs and is like a large crust that alters the "evidences" of those primary meanings, of those criteria. If we wish to contradict that layer deposited by society and its mentality, then we must challenge common opinion.

The most audacious challenge to that mentality that dominates us and touches us at every point – from our spiritual life to our clothing – is to become accustomed to making a judgment about everything in the light of our primary "evidences" and not at the mercy of our more occasional reactions. This judgment is all the more necessary because even these occasional opinions are induced by a context and a history, and they too must be transcended so that we can reach our original needs. For example, the way we conceive of the relationship between a man and a woman, although seen as something intimate and personal, is, in fact, widely determined by both our own instinctive disposition, which does not evaluate according to the original need of affection, and by the images of love created by public opinion. It is necessary to perforate always such images induced by the cultural climate in which we are immersed, to come down and grasp our own original needs and "evidences" and to judge and evaluate accordingly every proposal, every existential suggestion.

The use of elementary experience, or of one's own "heart" is, therefore, not popular especially when one comes face to face with onself. This "heart" is vulnerable, precisely the origin of that undefinable unease that overtakes the individual, when for example, he or she is treated as an object of another's interest or pleasure. Our own need as men and women is, however, different from this: we have need of love, and unfortunately, this is too easily altered.

Let us begin to judge. This is the beginning of liberation.

Recovering this existential depth permits this liberation; yet, in doing so an individual cannot avoid going against the current. We could call this *ascetic work,* where the word *ascesis* means man's work – man engaged directly on the path to his own destiny, seeking his own maturity. It is work, and it does not come naturally. It is simple and yet it is not to be taken for granted.

What has been said up to now must be rediscovered and reconquered. And even though in every era man has had to work to reconquer himself, we live in an age in which the need for this reconquest is clearer than ever.

In Christian terms, this labour is part of *metanoia,* or conversion.

2 The Second Premise: Reasonableness

Our first premise, the need for realism, has pointed to the primacy of the object: we have concluded that the method by which something is approached is determined by the object; it is not imagined at the subject's whim.

The second premise, on the other hand, singles out the acting subject, "man." By reasonableness I mean what this word says about a common experience. Even philosophers must use reasonableness in their everyday relations. In this sense, reasonableness means the realization of the value of reason in action. But even the term *reason* might easily be called into question. By reason, I mean the distinctive characteristic of that level of nature that we call man, that is, the capacity to become aware of reality according to the totality of its factors. The term *reasonableness,* then, represents a mode of action that expresses and realizes reason, the capacity to become aware of reality.

REASONABLENESS: A STRUCTURAL REQUIREMENT OF MAN

Let us, first of all, ask ourselves: How do we perceive whether or not an attitude is reasonable? Since reasonableness is a characteristic of our experience, it is only by observing our own experience that we can discover what such a characteristic implies, according to the principle of realism discussed in chapter one. The following examples will demonstrate this point.

Suppose a friend of ours, at a time of year far from Halloween, were to appear before us decked out in the helmet and a mail of a medieval knight. To our astonished questions, he might, in all seriousness, express the fear that one of the bystanders might want to attack him and that he has prepared himself for such an eventuality. We would feel that we are faced with an abnormality. To be sure, we would not perceive our friend's attitude as reasonable.

In another instance, I might present myself before an audience and place my briefcase on a table; if I should suddenly pick up the same briefcase and, with an energetic and well-aimed throw, pitch it out the window, the audience, if no other explanation should be offered, would consider my action unreasonable.

In both of these examples, the different actions appear unreasonable because they do not allow one to glimpse possible *reasons* for them. However, if I should throw my briefcase after four armed men had broken into the hall with their guns drawn, the audience would wonder what was in the briefcase, and my action would not be felt to be unreasonable. If later I also explained that the case contained a treasure of inestimable value, the spectators would see clearly the reasonableness of my deed, which, although formally identical to the preceding one, would be perceived by the audience as being supported with reasons.

Nor is this enough. I might approach the same audience and address it using a shipboard megaphone, explaining that I have brought the enormous instrument into the hall because I have lost my voice. My action would not be considered reasonable. Although I would have declared the reason for using the instrument – the loss of my voice – my listeners would not perceive it to be *adequate* because such an apparatus would seem out of place in an auditorium. However, using the same object on a ship would not raise a problem: although the reason would be the same, it would then match the circumstances.

Let us summarize. The same act in the first example – throwing the briefcase – seems unreasonable, that is, without reasons, and reasonable in the second, because it is understood that there are *reasons* for it. In the second example, to use a megaphone in an auditorium is judged unreasonable because, even though there is a reason, it is deemed to be *inadequate,* while to utilize the same instrument on a ship, even though the reason is identical, is perceived as proportionate and adequate. In experience, therefore, the reasonable appeals when man's behaviour shows itself to have *adequate reasons.*

If reason means becoming aware of reality, this cognitive relation with the real must develop in a reasonable way; that is, the steps for establishing this relationship must be determined by adequate motives.

This, from the point of view of the subject, is complementary to what we said about the object determining the method. We can say that the nature of the subject decides the way this method is used. And the nature of the subject is a being endowed with reason!

REDUCTIVE USE OF REASON

It is important not to limit the scope of the meaning of reasonableness.

a. The word rational is often identified with the term demonstrable in the strict sense of the word. Now, it is not true that the entire human experience of the reasonable is contained in this identification. Although it is certain that the reasonable seeks, desires, aspires, and is curious to demonstrate everything, it is not true that reasonable is identical with demonstrable: the capacity to demonstrate is an aspect of reasonableness, but the reasonable is not solely the capacity to demonstrate.

What does it mean to demonstrate? It means to retrace all of the steps of a process by which something comes into being. At school, if during a demonstration of a theorem, a step were skipped, the teacher would interrupt: "This has not been demonstrated." In fact, all of the steps constitutive of a reality have to be retraced before we can say that we have a demonstration.

But this does not exhaust the meaning of the term reasonable, because precisely the most interesting, original aspects of reality are not demonstrable: the process to which we have just referred cannot be applied to them. For example, man cannot demonstrate how things exist, but the answer to the question of how things exist is supremely interesting to him. Even if one should prove that this table is made of a material that has a given composition, he could never retrace all of the steps which brought this table into existence.

b. The reasonable cannot be identified with the "logical." Logic is an ideal of coherence; if you posit certain premises and develop them coherently, you will reach a logical outcome. If the premises are wrong, perfect logic will produce an erroneous result.

The truly interesting question for man is neither logic, a fascinating game, nor demonstration, an inviting curiosity. Rather, the intriguing problem for man is how to adhere to reality, to become aware of reality. This is a matter of being compelled by reality, not one of logical consistency. To acknowledge a mother's love for her child is not the conclusion of a logical process: it is evident, a certainty, or a proposal made by reality whose existence one must admit. The existence of the desk at which I work, my mother's attachment to me, even if they should not be logically developed conclusions, are realities that correspond to truth, and it is reasonable to affirm them. Logic, coherence, demonstration are no more than instruments of reasonableness at the service of a greater hand, the more ample "heart," that puts them to use.

Nota bene: I think it is important to concentrate our attention more on the word *reasonable* rather than on the term *reason.* Indeed, reason itself, this ability to become aware of reality, can be used in an unreasonable manner, that is, without adequate motives.

In any case, the root of the problem lies in the concept of *reason.* I would like to recount an event that happened to me years ago and from which I have learned much. I was about to teach a religion class in a classical lyceum for the first time. As soon as I had reached my desk and even before I had the chance to speak, I noticed a raised hand in the last row. I asked the student what he wanted. The answer, more or less, was the following: "Excuse me, Professor, but it is useless for you to come here and speak to us about faith, to reason about faith, because reason and faith represent two wholly different worlds. What can be said about faith has nothing to do with the exercise of reason and vice versa; therefore, to reason about faith is to engage in a mystification." I asked the student what faith meant to him, and, having received no answer, addressed the question to the whole class, with the same result. At that point, I asked the student in the last row to define reason and, at his silence, again posed the question to the rest of the class. Again I was met by silence. Then I said, "How can you form a judgment on faith and reason without first having tried to become aware of what they are? You use words whose meanings you have not grasped."

As might have been expected, my statement sparked a heated debate, and I became increasingly aware that the philosophy teacher had exerted a certain influence on these students. Leaving the room at the end of the class, I met that very teacher. Immediately, I told him I was astonished that the students thought it obvious that faith could have nothing to do with reason. His response was to state that the Church had affirmed the same thing at the Second Council of Orange.[1] I reminded him that every statement must be interpreted in the historical context from which it has arisen and whose views and concerns it expresses. To rip a sentence out of its cultural and literary context and to read it entirely as if it had been written in the present violates basic historical rules and does not allow for its correct understanding. At that point, the argument had widened, and the group of students surrounding us had become larger, and even though it was already time to move on to the next class, I wanted the students to understand the nature of the argument between the philosophy teacher and myself. I asked him, "Professor, I have never been to America, but I can assure you with certainty that America exists. I affirm this with the same certainty with which I state that you are before me at this very moment. Do you find my certainty reasonable?" After a few moments of silence and evident embarrassment, the answer was, "No." This was the point which I wanted to make clear to the students, and this is also what I want to clarify now: My concept of reason embraces the idea that it can be most reasonable to admit that America exists without ever having seen it; the other teacher's idea of reason, on the contrary, led him to state that this is not a reasonable position.

For me, reason is openness to reality, a capacity to seize and affirm it in all of its factors. For that other teacher, reason is the "measure" of things, and a phenomenon becomes true only when it can be directly demonstrated.

DIVERSITY OF PROCEDURES

What I am about to say will simply exemplify the systematic way in which human reason, becoming aware of reality proceeds using adequate motives.

If I say, $(a+b)\ (a-b) = a^2-b^2$, I affirm an algebraic or mathematical value, one belonging to the field of mathematical truths. And how do I arrive at the point of being able to claim that $(a+b)\ (a-b) = a^2-b^2$? I follow a certain path. I take steps on a road, hidden at first, as if by fog, one step after another, and finally, when the fog lifts, I am faced with the sight of truth, evidence, identity. I have taken a road, arrived at a certain point, where things have become evident and the truth is in sight. It is like going through a tunnel and reaching, at a given moment, a terrace from which I can look upon nature.

Let us examine two other examples. Water is H_2O. To reach this conclusion, I do not solve a mathematical problem. I analyze the components of water and note the result. In my third example, one can ask: "In relation to men, what rights do women have?" A human being has certain rights; a woman is a human being, therefore, she has the same rights as a man. I have not engaged in the resolution of elaborate mathematical formulas in order to understand that a woman has the same rights as a man; nor have I subjected the woman to a chemical analysis! Rather, I have followed a different path, and, at a given point, the syllogism has made the truth evident to me.

In Greek, the word for road is *hodos,* and "along the road," "by the road" is *met'hodon,* from which our word "method" is derived. *Method* comes from the Greek and *procedure* from the Latin. It is through a procedure (or "process') that I arrive at a knowledge of the object.

Reason, then, as the ability to become aware of reality or values, that is, of the real in so far as it enters the human horizon, follows different *methods* in order to come to know certain values or types of truth. Precisely because reason examines the object according to adequate motives or steps, it develops different paths, depending upon the object. (The method is imposed by the object!)

Reason is not as arthritic or paralyzed as has been imagined by so much of modern philosophy, which has reduced it to a single operation – "logic" – or to a specific type of phenomenon, to a certain capacity for "empirical demonstration." Reason is much larger than this; it is life, a life faced with the complexity and multiplicity of reality, the richness of the real. Reason is agile, goes everywhere, travels many roads. I have simplified in giving examples.

To employ reason is always a particular application of man's capacity to know. This capacity implies many methods, procedures, or processes depending upon the type of object in question. Reason does not have a single method; it is polyvalent, rich, agile, and mobile.

If this fundamental fact is not kept in mind, we risk falling into grave errors. Experts in a philosophical or theological method, if they claim to affirm a scientific truth, can make the same mistake as some gentlemen of the Holy Office did with Galileo Galilei: experts in theological exegesis tried to make the Bible say what it had no intention of saying. But the Bible in no way wanted to define the structure of the cosmos. It spoke according to the mentality of the people of the time, affirming religious and ethical values.

A PARTICULARLY IMPORTANT PROCEDURE

Imagine Peter, John, and Andrew before Jesus of Nazareth. They knew his mother, father, and relatives; they fished and ate with him. At some point, it became evident to them that they could say of that man: "If I should not believe this man, then I should not even believe my own eyes." Can this certainty be reasonable? If it can be so, what is the method that leads me to it? Let us remember that the method is no more than a description of reasonableness in the relation to the object. The method establishes the adequate reasons with which to take steps towards the knowledge of the object.

But this can be expressed in yet other ways. I can say with certainty, "My mother loves me." This is the most important aspect of motherhood because, if I had been abandoned when I was two months old and had been adopted by another woman, my mother would be the one who accepted me, if she loves me. "My mother is a woman who loves me." Of this I am as certain as of the light of the sun and even more confident than the fact that the earth turns around the sun, in the sense that this is of greater interest to me and is more important for my life. For my perception of the real, for my relationship with destiny, it is more significant that this woman should love me than to acquire the knowledge that the earth turns around the sun. It is very beautiful that we have discovered that the earth revolves around the sun, and not vice versa, because this is an aspect of the truth. However, as far as life is concerned, that is, the problem of my relation to destiny, this fact is not everything. Indeed, it has little to do with my problem as a whole.

One final example: I have in mind some people of whom I would say: "See, these are people who are friends, who are truly my friends." If I should be told to demonstrate it, what method could I use to do so? By reasoning about it? By the use of strange geometrical formulas? By the application of some scientific method? No. What was true about my mother's love is equally applicable to this situation.

There are realities, values which one cannot come to know utilizing the three methods we have mentioned. These are values that touch on human behaviour, not in its mechanical aspect, which can be identified with sociology or psychology, but with respect to its meaning, as the examples illustrate. Can you trust that man or not? Up to what point can you rely on him? What qualities can be valuable to you in another person? Is such and such a person loyal or not? The certain knowledge of these values cannot be acquired by the methods we have discussed. And yet, no one can deny that you can reach a reasonable certainty about them. One sphere of realities of which conscience can become aware, then, is that of "moral" realities or truths as defined in the etymological sense, that is, in so far as they describe human "behaviour," which, in Latin, is called "mores."

In the search for truths and certainties about human behaviour, reason must be used in a different way; otherwise it is no longer reasonable. To claim to define human behaviour using a scientific method would not be an adequate procedure. A few examples should suffice to illustrate this point.

Imagine that I went to my mother's tonight and found that she prepared a delicious supper for me. Suppose, instead of throwing myself at the plate, famished, I simply stared at the food. She would ask, "Do you not feel well?" To which I would answer, "I feel fine, but I would very much like to analyze this food to make sure it is not poisoned." Naturally, my mother would reply, "You are always kidding!" On the other hand, if she thought that my remark was serious, she would not call in a chemist, but a psychiatrist. I do not have to submit the food in question to a chemical analysis to be sure that my mother does not intend to poison me.

Let us also suppose that I should meet a friend at a streetcar stop. "Hello!" I call out to him. "Hello! How are you?" he replies. He gets on the streetcar, but I stay behind. When the car begins to move, my friend sticks his head out of the window and asks, "Why didn't you get on?" And I answer, "As long as the transit authority does not psychologically examine its drivers at every stop, I am no longer using streetcars." That streetcar would take a year to cross the city!

Mathematics, the sciences, and philosophy are necessary for the evolution of man as history. They are fundamental conditions for civilization. But one could live very well without philosophy or without knowing that the earth revolves around the sun. Man cannot live, however, without moral certainties, without being able to form sure judgments about the behaviour of others toward him. This is so true that uncertainty in relationships is one of the most terrible afflictions of our generation. It is difficult to become certain about relationships, even within the family. We live as if we were seasick, with such insecurity in the fabric of our relations that we no longer build what is human. We might construct skyscrapers, atomic bombs, the most subtle systems of philosophy, but we no longer build the human because it consists of relationships.

This is why nature, in certain fields, has created a method, a path, a type of slow development to arrive at certain truths. We must take all of the steps in a fixed way; otherwise we are unsure of being able to proceed. Consequently, some truths are reached only after centuries and even millennia. On the other hand, to arrive at certainties about relationships we have been given the fastest of methods, almost more like an intuition than a process. This fourth method is much closer to the artist's approach than to the technician's or the demonstrator's, because man needs it to live in the instant.

One method produces mathematical certainty, another scientific, and yet another philosophical; the fourth method yields certainties about human behaviour, "moral" certainties. I have stated that, as a method, the last one is closer to the approach of the artist or the genius, who, through signs, proceeds to the perception of the true. When Newton saw the famous apple fall, it became a *sign* that immediately produced his great hypothesis. Genius needs only a small indication to reach a universal intuition. The method by which I understand that my mother loves me and through which I am certain that many people are my friends cannot be fixed mechanically; my intelligence intuits that the only reasonable meaning, the only reasonable interpretation of the convergence of a given set of "signs" is this. If these signs, in their hundreds and thousands, could be indefinitely multiplied, their only adequate meaning would be that my mother loves me. Thousands of indications converge on this point: my mother's behaviour only means this: "my mother loves me."

The demonstration of a moral certainty is the consequence of a complex of indications whose only adequate meaning – whose only adequate motive and whose only reasonable reading – is that certainty itself. This is called not just a moral certainty, but also an *existential certainty*, because it is bound to the moment at which you examine the phenomenon, that is, when you intuit all of the signs. An example: I am not worried that the person now in front of me may want to kill me; not even after this statement does this person want to kill me, if only for the satisfaction of proving that I am wrong. I reach this conclusion by reading certain facets of his behaviour and a specific situation. But I could not be as certain about the future, when the circumstances might be very different.

Two important points:

The first: I will be able to be certain about you, to the extent that I pay more attention to your life, that is, that I share in your life. The signs leading to certainty become multiplied in the measure in which you pay attention to them. For example, in the Gospel, who was able to understand the need to trust that man? Not the crowd looking for a cure, but those who followed him and shared his life. Life together (*convivenza*) and shared!

The second: inversely, the more powerfully one is human, the more one is able to become certain about another on the basis of only a few indications. This is the human genius, the genius that is able to read the truth of behaviour, of man's way of life. The more powerfully human one is, the more one is able to perceive with certainty. "To trust is good, but not to trust is better." This proverb offers a rather superficial kind of wisdom because the capacity to trust another is proper to the strong and secure man. The insecure man does not even trust his own mother. The more one is truly human, the more one is able to trust, because one understands the reasons for believing in another. To express this in another way, one who has a "knack" for a certain subject needs only a clue to intuit the solution to the problem, while everyone else has to work labouriously through every step. To have a "knack" for something is like having a certain affinity for it. The knack for being human entails possessing much humanity; it is then that I can know up to what point I can trust in your humanity. In applying this method, it is as if one makes a fast comparison with oneself, with one's own "elementary experience," with one's own "heart," and says: "Up to this point, what I see corresponds with my heart, with those needs and evidences, with what I was made for; therefore, it is true, and I can trust this other human being."

AN APPLICATION OF THE METHOD OF MORAL CERTAINTY: FAITH

What is faith? It is an adhesion to what another affirms. This may be unreasonable, if there are no adequate reasons; if there are, it is reasonable. If I have reached the certainty that another person knows what he says and does not mislead me, then to repeat with certainty what he has affirmed with certainty, is to be consistent with myself. It is exactly through this process of moral certainty that I can reach conclusions about the sincerity and capacity of another person.

Without this cognitive method of faith, there would be no human development. If the only reasonableness consisted in evidence that was immediate or personally demonstrated (as was the contention of the teacher of philosophy regarding America), man could no longer move forward because each of us would have to go through all of the processes again; we would always be cavemen.

In this sense, the question of moral certainty is the main problem of life as existence, but, through it, also of life as civilization and culture, because all that is produced by the other three methods we mentioned can become the basis for a new thrust forward only on the strength of this fourth method.

I hope it has become evident why, in this premise, I focused on the necessity for reasonableness. The object of a study requires realism: the method is imposed by the object; but, concomitantly and complementarily with this, it is necessary that the application of this method respect the need for reasonableness which is proper to man's nature. And reasonableness means having adequate motives in every step we take toward the object of our knowledge. The diversity of methods establishes their order. A method is a locus of adequate motives.

It would be unreasonable to require that, in order to be sure about man's behaviour, scientific criteria had to be applied and that, if these could not, a certainty could not be reached. This position is unreasonable because it is not based upon adequate motives, as our observation of experience has illustrated.

Conversely, certainty about human behaviour may be well founded and, therefore, completely reasonable. Our life is made up of this type of reasonableness. I speak of our most interesting life, that of relationships, but also, in the end, of that life of relationships that establishes history and by which even discoveries made by other methods are handed down.

Finally, let us note that man can err using the scientific, philosophical, or mathematical methods. In the same way, he can misjudge human behaviour. This does not detract from the fact that certainties may be reached by the scientific method and, in the same way, through the method of "moral" knowledge.

3 The Third Premise:
The Impact of Morality
on the Dynamic of Knowing

The first premise insisted on the necessity for realism; realism is imposed by the nature and the situation of the object. The second premise emphasized concern and love for rationality, and this was intended to bring to light the acting subject, and the manner of the subject's movements. But, in facing a question such as, "How can one trust another person?" a problem still remains that does not depend upon the soundness of the reasoning process. Trusting another person introduces a new factor, namely, the attitude of the person – usually called "morality." The third premise seeks then to address the impact of morality on the dynamic of knowing.

REASON INSEPARABLE FROM THE UNITY OF THE "I"

A certain young woman is very good at math. One day she has a test in class. She has a bad stomachache and, on that morning, she does not do well on the exam. Has she suddenly become ignorant? No, she simply has a stomachache.

A particular young man writes well. He will surely become a journalist. One night he goes over to the house of some friends where they are serving some venison and excellent wine. The young man eats and drinks with a robust appetite until he is nearly bursting, and that night he becomes very ill. It is very likely that the composition he will write the next morning will not represent his best literary exploit. He puts together a piece that is just barely passable. Has he suddenly lost his spirit? No, the poor fellow simply has indigestion.

We can see from these examples that there is a *profound unity,* an organic relationship, between the instrument of reason and the rest of the person. Man is one, and reason is not a machine that can be disconnected from the rest of the personality and then left to operate alone like some spring mechanism in a toy. Reason is inherent in the entire unity of our self; it is organically related to it. That is why we cannot reason well in the presence of physical pain, anger, or disappointment or when others do not appear to understand us or our orientation. For instance, this same young man, who is angry because his parents do not understand him, will reason less well during an exam. If his long-time girlfriend left him – treacherously and without notice only because she happened to meet someone else – he would be alone, listless, frozen, and his state of soul could be such that he would no longer be balanced in using his rational instruments.

Let us establish first of all, then, that reason is not some mechanism that can be separated from man – just as a saddle cannot be stripped from a horse as it gallops along the road, so is reason profoundly and organically related to the entire "self."

REASON BOUND TO FEELING

I will begin this section with a few illustrations. The first case: A skier loses consciousness following a spectacular fall. He comes to in a spotless hospital room and, upon awakening, becomes immediately aware of a terrific pain: he has broken his collarbone.

The second case: For a student writing a class composition, time passes without results. After forty-five minutes of fruitless agony, a great idea suddenly pops into his mind, and he eagerly grabs a piece of paper and starts writing and writing.

The third case: A young woman walking down the street hears someone behind her hissing "psst, psst," trying to get her attention. There are three possibilities: "It's that pest again!", or "Now who could that be?", or her heart beats more violently because she knows who it is.

Now, these phenomena have a common denominator: something always has an impact on the individual's sphere of experience. An event penetrates one's personal experience, whether it be physical (the broken collarbone), mental (an idea realized), or an affective emotion (nuisance, curiosity, pleasure); within the experiential sphere, the confines of a person's perceptions, something happens, something penetrates and, inevitably, mechanically produces a certain reaction: a physical pain, an emotional state such as happiness, or curiosity, etc. which touches or "moves" the person.

Let us expand this observation and generalize upon it: anything that has an impact on a person's sphere of knowledge produces an inevitable and irresistible reaction, its magnitude depending upon the measure of the person's human vivacity. This reaction might be a "state of soul," whereby the person may become indifferent, sympathetic, or antipathetic or any possible nuance of these words: but the point is that there exists nothing that enters our sphere of knowledge – and, therefore, our experience – that does not provoke, stir up, solicit, determine, and thus establish within us a certain "state of soul."

There is a word that expresses this "state of soul," this reaction, this emotion, this state of being whereby we are touched by something that happens to us; it is called *feeling*. Depending upon the measure of the individual's human vivacity, anything whatsoever that enters his personal horizon (even a single blade of grass, or a pebble that you kick with your foot) moves him, touches him, provokes a reaction: this reaction can differ in its nature or type, but it is always a certain specific feeling.

Man is that level of nature where nature itself becomes conscious of itself, that level of reality where reality begins to become aware of itself, begins to become reason. Now if we apply the term "value" to the object of knowledge, in so far as it interests the life of reason, value, then, is known reality in as much as it interests us, as it has worth. If someone has a narrow mind and a small, mean heart, he will find much less value in the world around him than a person who has a great soul, who is vivacious. The Gospel reminds us that for our Lord even a small flower in the field, which man tramples upon without being aware, is valuable; indeed, he adds, that even Solomon, in all of his glory, was not able to adorn himself as splendidly as the Father in heaven adorns that little flower (Matt. 6:28–9). Therefore, depending upon a person's individual position and temperament, a known object touches him, provoking that emotion that we have identified with the word feeling. We can thus say that *feeling* is the inevitable "state of soul" that follows upon the knowledge of anything passing across or penetrating the horizon of our experience.

But, we must be cautious here for, as we have said, reason is not just some mechanism that can be detached from the rest of our "self." Rather, reason is related to our feeling and conditioned by it as well. Hence, we reach this definitive formula: in order for reason to know an object, it must also take into account feeling, the "state of soul," by which it is filtered and with which it is, in any case, involved.

THE HYPOTHESIS OF REASON WITHOUT INTERFERENCE

Here we arrive at a question tied to modern rationalistic and enlightenment culture that is also easily accepted as a common characteristic of our day-to-day mentality.

Reason is thought of as a capacity for knowing an object in such a way that nothing should interfere. If, then, something else does intervene, such as one's "state of soul" or feeling, then the question is asked, "Can this knowledge be objective, a true knowledge of the object, or is it not wholly or partially an impression of the subject?"

The discussion assumes a more dramatic flavour if we add this further observation. Man cannot avoid being interested in the meaning of things. I am speaking of those things that engage man in his search for personal meaning or which claim to contain his own significance. I would say that such objects of knowledge might fall into three categories: the problem of destiny, the affective problem, and the political problem.

The more something interests an individual, that is to say, the more *value* it has (worth for a person's life), the more vital it is (that is, interests life), the more powerfully will it generate a state of soul, a reaction of antipathy or sympathy – "feeling" – and the more forcefully will reasoning, in the act of knowing that value in relation to our lives, be conditioned by this feeling. Thus our rationalistic culture can say: "It is clear that objective certainty cannot be reached when dealing with these types of phenomena because the factor of feeling plays too large a role. All questions concerning destiny, love, social, and political life and its ideals are a matter of opinion because one's personal position in its mechanical aspect as a state of soul and feeling plays too large a role."

If we call r (or reason) the human subject's cognitive energy and if we call v (or value) the reality to be known in so far as it succeeds in penetrating the sphere of human interest, then, according to the position we are looking at, r will never be able to have a clear and objective idea of v, due to the intermediary and modifying presence of f (or feeling). Thus we arrive at the following formula:

$$r \rightarrow f \leftarrow v$$

The object of knowledge, in as much as it interests us (v), evokes a state of feeling (f) that conditions the capacity for knowledge (r). The serious use of reason would require either that f be eliminated or reduced to a bare minimum. Only by its removal, or, if we will, the drastic reduction of the factor *f*, can knowledge be truly objective – true knowledge of the object.

But where, in reality, can we take such a precaution? Only in science and mathematics. Therefore – the proponents of such a hypothesis argue – only in the field of science and mathematics can the truth about an object be perceived and affirmed. With any other type of knowledge – concerning destiny, the affective and political problems – one can never reach objective certainty, a true knowledge of the object. These matters are the undisputed territory of opinion and subjective impression.

AN EXISTENTIAL QUESTION AND A QUESTION OF METHOD

Two observations must be made concerning this matter.

a. First, existentially, if this position were pushed to its logical limit, it would conclude: the more nature arouses my interest in something, the more it makes me curious, gives me the need and passion to know that thing, and the more it prevents me from knowing it. Indeed, as soon as nature endows me with an interest in an object, it conditions my capacity to know it by the feeling that is produced. Now it is true that the great poet Giacomo Leopardi exclaimed "O nature, nature / ... / why do you deceive your children so?"[1] However, this was an explosion of bitterness, of existential sadness. It cannot be established as the principle of a philosophical position. Our entire being rebels against such a stance. Certainly, nature could turn out to be irredeemably contradictory. But before settling upon such a conclusion, it is reasonable to search for some other solution. And it is toward just such a solution that we are setting out.

b. Second, in order to resolve this problem, it is erroneous to formulate an explanatory principle that will eliminate one of the factors involved. This is quite simply not a valid principle: if nature makes us this way, why should we have to arrive at an explanation or solution for this problem or enigma by saying, "Let's suppress one of the elements of the problem?" Doing so is not reasonable. The true solution lies in a position that not only does not feel the need to eliminate one factor or another, but highlights and values all factors.

ANOTHER POINT OF VIEW

In our case, if we look carefully, we can easily find this other point of view, an adequate and balanced frame of mind able to value our human dynamism in its entirety.

Let us imagine for a moment that we are on vacation in Val Gardena, a valley high in the Alps. At a certain point, we come to Sella Pass. It is a splendid day. I take out a pair of binoculars and try to look around, but I cannot see a thing. Everything is dark and opaque. Then I focus the lens and am presented with an exceptional panorama, so clear that I can even make out some people skiing on Marmolada, the highest mountain around. The lenses of the binoculars are not made to block my view or make it more difficult to see, but to make it easier. So how do they do this? By, so to speak, carrying Marmolada closer to the pupil of my eye, so that the "seeing energy" of my eye, if you will, grasps it more easily. Nature has placed a small lens within my eye, not to impede the visual energy of my optic nerve, but, on the contrary, to facilitate the task. In fact, it is as if the lens brought the objects closer so that the visual energy of my eye can "seize" them.

This can serve as an analogy for the problem that concerns us here. Let us imagine f, or feeling, as a kind of lens; the object is carried closer to a person's cognitive energy by this lens so that reason can know it more easily and securely. The f is, therefore, an important condition for knowledge. Feeling is an essential factor for seeing – not in the sense that it itself sees, but in the sense that it represents the condition by which the eye, or our reason, sees in accordance with its nature.

This explanation values all three factors – reason, value, and feeling – and seems to me simply rational. If an individual has a cataract in his eye and his vision is impaired, or if the lens of the eye is too flat or too convex and no longer sees properly, either up close or far away, the point is not to rip the lens from the eye, but for the lens to be *focused*!

Feeling, then, must not be eliminated, but it must be in *its proper place.*

It may seem correct from a purely abstract point of view that man, when he judges something, should be absolutely neutral or altogether indifferent toward the object he judges. However, this cannot work well when vital values are involved. It is truly a mystification – not a utopia – to imagine that a judgment (the attempt to reach the truth of the object) made when one's state of soul is perfectly untouched and completely indifferent is more worthy and valid. First of all, making such "indifferent" judgments is, above all, impossible, due to the very structure of human dynamism. The impact of feeling does not diminish, but increases where the object becomes more filled with meaning. Besides, judging a proposal regarding the meaning of our lives with absolute indifference would be like treating the problem as one would treat a rock. And, under those circumstances, one normally cannot understand anything any more.

Now, what does it mean to "focus the lens," or to "put our feeling in its proper place"? First of all, it is clear that such a problem is not scientific, but concerns attitude; that is to say, it is a "moral" problem, dealing with an individual's way of handling, controlling himself, how he places himself before reality. It is not a problem of acumen or intelligence.

I would like to make an historical comparison. Christopher Columbus and Galileo Galilei revolutionized the way in which we look at geography and astronomy. Their work is among the culminating moments in the transitions that drive forward history, culture, and civilization. Another great name is Louis Pasteur: the discovery of the role of microorganisms in medicine really revolutionized everything. Pasteur had to repeat his experiments again and again because it seemed that no one was able to recognize their value. The professors at the Sorbonne, members of the Academy of Science in Paris, were the very last to acknowledge their scientific validity. For these men, to admit the soundness of Pasteur's claims would mean going up to the podium the next day and announcing that much had to change – pride, fame, and money were all in the way. The problem of how microbes function, which is an objective, scientific problem, was for them vital. What would those professors have needed to be able to perceive for themselves the value of these experiments, which were irrefutable even to the uninitiated? They would have needed a certain loyalty, a moral dignity, a passion for the true objective: these are the fruits of a long and moral education which these individuals could not have invented by themselves on the spur of the moment.

To summarize: if a certain thing does not interest me, then I do not look at it; if I do not look at it, then I cannot know it. In order to know it, I need to give my attention to it. In its Latin root, attention means "to be tensed toward ..." If it interests me, strikes me, I will be "tensed toward" it when faced with it.

We can observe that we study something that does not interest us only with difficulty. This can be a sign of narrow-mindedness; but it would certainly be a grave injustice to claim that we can judge it in the same way. Listen to the following example. Let us say that Mark and I are walking along the city streets. Because Mark has raised a serious problem, I am knocking myself out trying to explain things to him. He listens to me, and I grow ever more impassioned and ever more lucid – or so it seems to me – as I present my arguments. "So then, do you understand?" "Yes, yes, up to this point I follow you." We have been walking along talking, with our eyes fixed on the side walk.

But he lifts his eyes to notice a pretty woman walking on the other side of the street. He continues to say, "yes, yes," but in an increasingly mechanical manner as he fixes his eyes upon the lovely figure and turns his head to watch her as she moves away. This continues until she disappears in the distance. Discontentedly he withdraws his gaze and turns back to me in the very instant in which I have concluded my argument. I say to him, "So then, Mark, do you agree?" And he says, "No, no! I am not persuaded!"

This reply is not valid because he did not pay attention to my arguments. This is the offense that the majority of people commit when they face the problems of destiny, faith, religion, the Church, and Christianity because, being "anxious and troubled with many other things," in these things their minds are "dead and buried."[2] But then they claim to be able to pronounce a judgment, to have an opinion, partly because it is impossible not to have a viewpoint on these matters. A son cannot but have an opinion about his father and mother. So it is with any person who lives; he or she cannot escape having a view concerning the connection between his or her present and destiny.

It seems evident to me, from the example about Pasteur and the more banal one just mentioned, that the heart of the problem of human knowledge does not lie in a particular intellectual capacity. The more a value is vital and elementary in its importance – destiny, affection, common life – the more our nature gives to each of us the intelligence to know and judge it. The centre of the problem is really a proper position of the heart, a correct attitude, a feeling in its place, a morality.

THE MORALITY OF KNOWING

If morality means having the correct attitude, it is also determined by the object in question. For example, if one person has to teach and another works as a teller in a post office, the first should be moral in teaching and the second in receiving money and putting it into the appropriate accounts: these are two different dynamics. Even morality has a diversified dynamic. Now what application of morality are we discussing? Here we are talking about having a suitable attitude *in the dynamic of knowing* an object. We want to describe what morality consists of in so far as the dynamic of knowing is concerned.

I will expand upon this further. If an object does not interest me, I will leave it alone, and be more than content with a certain impression of it transmitted out of the corner of my eye. But in order to give an object my attention, I must make some sort of judgment about it, I must take it into consideration and, to do so, I insist, I must possess a certain interest in it. What does this interest mean? It means I must have a desire to know what the object *truly is.*

This may seem banal, but it is easier said than done. We are too readily interested in merely holding on to and reinforcing the opinions we already have about things, especially some things more than others. More precisely, we are inclined to remain bound to the opinions we already have about the *meaning* of things and to attempt to justify our attachment to them.

A small example will illustrate my point. When a young man has fallen in love with a young woman, if his mother, trying to be objective and sincere, draws his attention to some of her faults, the young man tends not to pay attention to her viewpoint, throwing at her this or that argument that will reinforce his own opinion about the young woman.

Applying this to the field of knowledge, this is the moral rule: *Love the truth of an object more than your attachment to the opinions you have already formed about it.* More concisely, one could say, "love the truth more than yourself."

I now propose a dramatic example: From the point of view of the intellectual environment, like the one created by power, and by the supreme instrument of power, namely, the dominant culture as it has existed from the middle of the nineteenth century on, let us try to discuss what the state of affairs is with regard to God, religiosity, and Christianity. We are all bursting with opinions in this regard, which have entered into our consciousness by a quasi osmosis or by a more explicit violence, imposed by the environment. To make true judgments on these matters – what a wrenching away it requires, what a labourious task to liberate ourselves, to break our attachment to impressions already acquired!

This is a problem of morality. The more vital a value, the more it is by its nature a proposal for life, the more the problem lies not in intelligence, but in morality, that is, a greater love for the truth than oneself. Concretely, morality is the sincere desire to know the object in question *in a true way,* beyond our attachment to our own opinions or those inculcated upon us. Dostoyevsky once said, "... if it were mathematically proved to you that truth was outside Christ, you would rather remain with Christ than with truth."[3] This sentence paradoxically expresses Dostoyevsky's profound attachment, esteem, and deep love for the figure of Christ. But as the sentence reads, literally, it is not a truly Christian statement which would, on the contrary, proclaim: I adhere to Christ because he is the truth.

In the Gospel, there is a sentence that expresses the same ethical imperative in a more fascinating way: "Blessed are the poor in spirit: the reign of God is theirs" (Matt. 5:3). But who are the poor? The poor are those who have nothing to defend, who are detached from those things that they seem to possess, so that their lives are not dedicated to affirming their own possession. The individual who is supremely poor in spirit is the one who, in the face of the truth, desires truth and nothing else, beyond all attachment that one may live, feel, undergo, and experience, beyond all devotion to the images that one has already formed about things.

The Lord gave an example, a paradigm of this attitude of love for the truth: "I assure you, unless you change and become like little children, you will not enter the Kingdom of God" (Matt. 18:3). He is not proposing an idea of infantility to us, but one of active sincerity in front of the real, before the object taken into consideration. Children have their eyes wide open. They do not say, "However ... , if ..., but ... ." Rather, they say, "black is black and white is white." As Christ again affirms, "Say 'Yes' when you mean 'Yes' and 'No' when you mean 'No.' Anything beyond that is from the evil one" (Matt. 5:37).

PRECONCEPTION

This corollary on "preconception" will anticipate something we will return to at greater length.

Now, it is clear that to love the truth more than our ideas about it is the same as being free of any preconception. However, "to be free of preconceptions" is an equivocal phrase, and, in the literal sense of the word, it is quite impossible. After all, by the very fact that we are born into a certain family, spend time with particular friends, have this or that teacher in grammar school, attend a certain junior high school, high school and university, watch television, read the newspaper, by the very fact that we are normal people living in normal conditions, we are entirely involved, as if by osmosis, with preconceptions – with ideas and images about values, about the meaning of things, especially in the three areas I have already mentioned: destiny, affectivity, and politics.

The real point, then, is not to be without preconceptions. On the contrary, I repeat: to the degree that a person is fruitful, powerful, and alive, so will that same person upon confronting situations, immediately react, form a judgment, and an image of things. The point is, rather, to cultivate that great and yet most simple detachment from oneself about which the Gospel teaches. When the Gospel speaks of this "detachment from oneself" (see Luke 17:33), it does not intend to claim that we should become removed from ourselves in the literal sense of the word. Rather, it encourages us to strive for an attitude with which we reflect upon our freedom and use its energy in a way that is true to its purpose.

At the end of the first premise, we concluded that in order to arrive at the source of criteria, which we called elementary experience, we need an ascetical labour, because we must always pass beyond a certain incrustation that life deposits upon us. And so now I say, in order to love the truth more than we love ourselves, in order to love the truth of the object more than the image that we have formed of it, to acquire a poverty of spirit, to have eyes that confront reality and truth wide open, like the eyes of children, there must be a process and *work*.

Here, as well, the painful process is called *ascesis*. Morality springs forth within us as something spontaneous. It is an original attitude. However, immediately thereafter, if it is not continually rejuvenated by work, it spoils, it becomes corrupt. The parabola with its trajectory tending inexorably toward corruption continually needs to be put back on course.

But what can persuade us to engage in this *ascesis*, this labour and this training? Man is, in fact, moved solely by love and affection. It is primarily the *love of ourselves as destiny*, the affection for our own *destiny* that can convince us to undertake this work to become habitually detached from our own opinions and our own imaginations (not to eliminate but to detach ourselves from them!), so that all of our cognitive energy will be focused upon a search for the truth of the object, no matter what it should be. This love is the ultimate inner movement, the supreme emotion that persuades us to seek true virtue.

4 The Religious Sense: The Starting Point

All we have said until now has not been for the sake of pure analytical curiosity. We have discussed these matters in order to call our attention to the conditions which must be respected when one approaches the problem of our religious sense, and they can be summarized within a single phrase: one must be open to the demands imposed by the question itself.

Let us now go to the heart of our argument, while at the same time keeping in mind a certain methodological consideration – we are made for truth, and truth is the correspondence between reality and consciousness. We already have described this as the nature of our rational dynamism. It is also worthwhile to restate that our search for the ultimate meaning of our lives is not a matter of a particular intelligence, or some special effort, or even exceptional means. Rather, finding the ultimate truth is like discovering something beautiful along one's path. One sees and recognizes it, if one is attentive. The issue, then, is this attention.

HOW TO PROCEED

How do we confront the religious experience so that we take in all of its constitutive factors? Let us now define our method. Although this may still seem like a preliminary step, it defines and clarifies the objective.

a) If the religious experience is an experience, then we must begin with ourselves in order to look at it in the face and to take in all of its essential aspects. Although one may object that such an observation seems rather self evident, still, by carefully and slowly examining this matter, I hope to show that the facts prove otherwise. Indeed, today's predominant mentality totally obliterates these very affirmations. Therefore, if one is speaking of an experience, then the starting point is oneself.

b) Nonetheless, "starting with one's self" is a proposition that can lead to equivocation. Perhaps the following will clarify my point. If we ask: "How do I identify myself?" this "myself" runs the risk of being defined by my own self images and preconceptions, which may also be abstract. So then when do we really begin with ourselves? To use oneself as a starting point is realistic when the person watches himself *in action,* in his or her daily experience. In fact, there simply does not exist a "self" abstracted from the actions the person performs, except in sleep – that strange, humoristic, and dramatic period into which man must nightly fall – because the individual is always in action. Therefore, starting with oneself means to observe one's own movements, taken off guard, within his or her daily experience. Hence the "material" of our starting point will not be any sort of preconception about or artificial image of oneself, or even a definition of oneself, perhaps borrowed from current ideas and the dominant ideology.

THE "I"-IN-ACTION

By observing ourselves in action, the factors which constitute us emerge and it is here that the most important characteristics of the human being appear. St Thomas says in his *De Veritate:* "In hoc aliquis percepit se animam habere et vivere et esse, quod percepit, se sentire et intelligence alia huiusmodi opera vitae exercere."[1] In other words, from this the individual understands that he exists – that he lives – by the fact that he thinks, feels, and performs other similar activities.

This statement is loaded with implications! A man who is truly and seriously lazy – not in the sense of the "leisure" that Jacques Leclercq eulogized,[2] but who although capable of a "ten" performance, gives a zero or one instead – this man is unable to understand himself, or, at best, is able to do so only with great difficulty.

Perhaps a few examples will illustrate my point. Let us imagine, for instance, a boy who, for whatever reason, does not like math and who has, therefore, never really studied it. This boy will not be in any position to know whether or not he at least has a normal aptitude for this field. If, on the other hand, he were to begin to apply himself, then he might even discover that he has a capacity that is well above the norm. This is because it is in action alone that one "discovers" this talent, this human factor. In another case, a fifteen or sixteen year old girl might begin a normal day saying to herself, "I'm worthless, I don't know how to do anything." If, however, by the evening of that same day a young man, whom she likes, were to have finally held her and said, "I love you," she would discover her self to be a different person than her dejection of the morning had led her to believe. The factors of her personality emerged by being provoked into an involvement.

It is for this reason that in our society unemployed people suffer a terrible assault upon their self-consciousness. In such conditions, their perception of their personal self-worth becomes increasingly clouded.

But attitudes analogous to the "I am not able" expressed by the girl in the example are not limited to adolescents. An adult, when confronted with a religious fact, assumes just such a position when he or she claims: "I don't feel God, and I have no need to confront this problem." In such a circumstance, the person takes on an attitude which is guided not by reason, but distracting centrifugal conditionings. Reason, if correctly applied, would not be able to eliminate such a problem. Instead these conditionings – used as abilis – lead to conclusions which have nothing at all to do with the reasonable formulation of a judgment, a judgment born of a real involvement with a fact most important to one's life.

As affirmed earlier, the factors that constitute humanity are perceived when they are engaged in action – otherwise they are not noticeable. It is as if they did not exist, as if they had been obliterated. Thus someone who has never wished to commit himself to the religious dimension within his life would be right in saying that this matter does not affect him. He would be correct because, as he has never involved himself in it, at a certain point, it is as if it did not exist for him. Of course, on the one hand, you could say that this person has assumed this position, without ever having brought into the horizon of his or her reason the elements necessary to make a judgment. On the other hand, for that person to have been conditioned in such a way, it was necessary for him to go through – as we shall see later – a complete and unreasonable course of forgetfulness.

INVOLVEMENT WITH LIFE

From our discussion so far, it becomes clear that the more one is involved with life, the more one also, even within a single experience, comes to know the very factors of life itself.

Life is a web of events and encounters which provoke the conscience, producing all different kinds of problems. But a problem is nothing other than the dynamic expression of a reaction in the face of these encounters. Life, then, is a series of problems, its fabric made up of reactions to encounters that are provocative to a greater or lesser extent. Discovering the meaning of life – or the most pertinent and important things in life – is a goal which is possible only for the individual who is involved with life seriously, its events, encounters, and problems.

Being involved with life does not mean an exasperated entanglement with one or another of life's aspects; it is never partial. Rather, one must live one's engagement with life's various facets as a consequence of a global involvement with life itself. Otherwise, one's engagement risks being partial, without equilibrium, existence possibly becoming a fixation or an hysteria. To paraphrase a saying of Chesterton, "Error is a truth gone mad."[3] Therefore, this involvement is the attitude required for our procedure to really work, and should not be confused with the kind of involvement that has for its objective only one or another aspect of existence.

In order for us to be able to discover within ourselves the existence and nature of such a crucial and decisive a factor as the religious sense, we must commit ourselves to our whole life. This includes everything – love, study, politics, money, even food and rest, excluding nothing, neither friendship, nor hope, nor pardon, nor anger, nor patience. Within every single gesture lies a step towards our own destiny.

ASPECTS OF THE INVOLVEMENT

a) One essential aspect of life, one of the elements crucial to our involvement with our entire existence, is *tradition*. This essential component of our existence is normally overlooked, forgotten, at least on a conscious level, and its value is even denigrated and disfigured.

Tradition is strongly connected to the religious problem. Indeed, the religious factor unifies the past, present, and future. And when it is authentic, it is profoundly a friend and appraiser of every nuance of the past. It is likewise ready to risk anything for the future, and, for the present, as the Gospel says, it is indomitable, unsleeping, and vigilant (Luke 21:36).

Each one of us is born into a certain tradition. Nature casts us into the dynamic of existence, arming us with this complex instrument with which we can confront our surroundings. Every man and woman faces his or her external reality endowed by nature with elements that one finds in oneself as given, already offered. Tradition is that complex endowment with which nature arms us.

We do not possess tradition in order to become fossilized within it, but to develop it, even to the point of profoundly changing it. But in order to transform it, we must first of all act "with" what has been given to us; we must use it. And it is through the values and richness which I have received that I can become, in my own turn, creative, capable not only of developing what I find in my hands, but also changing radically both its meaning, its structure, and perspective.

We can visualize tradition as a work plan with which nature equips us as it sets us down into this great construction site of life and history. Only by putting this working hypothesis into action can we begin, not simply to gasp for air, but, with our reasoned judgments, our projects, and our critical outlook to have an impact on our surroundings and therefore on that extremely interesting factor which is part of those surroundings, ourselves. Hence it is urgent to be loyal to tradition: it is a requirement for a complete involvement with existence.

Let us say that a man is launched on life's path with a tradition in his hands. Suppose he throws it away before putting it to use with a loyalty coming right from the very core of his being, before having really verified it. His refusal of something so inherent to his nature would betray a fundamental disloyalty in other aspects of his life as well, particularly with respect to himself and his own destiny.

In order that this loyalty to tradition become a truly active working hypothesis, one must apply this traditional richness to the problem of life through the critical principle referred to in our first premise as elementary experience. When this critical principle is omitted, the subject is either alienated by or fossilized within his tradition or, sold into the violence of his environment, he will end up abandoning it. As is the case for most people concerning their religious consciousness, this is all the more true: the violence of their surroundings decides for them.

I insist then upon this point: using tradition critically does not mean doubting its value – even if this is what is suggested by the current mentality. Rather, it means using this incredibly rich working hypothesis by filtering it through this *critical principle* which is inherent within us: elementary experience. If tradition is critically used in such a manner, then it becomes a facet of our personality, the material for a specific face, an identity, an identity in the world. Goethe used to say: "Was du ererbt von deinen Vatern hast, erwirb es, um es zu besitzen"[4] ("what from thy sires inherited thou hast / acquire it, if thou wouldst possess it").

b) A second aspect of the commitment of the self, fundamental to discovering the facets which constitute it, is the value of the *present*.

Starting from the present is inevitable. In order to deepen our outlook of the past – whether it be the near or distant past – from which point do we start? From the present. In order to venture into risky visions of the future, what is the starting point? The present.

At first, this barely perceptible present appears to our eyes to be nothing, only an instant, but when you look at it, it appears so full and brimming with all that has preceded us! In the measure in which I am myself, I am replete with all that has preceded me. Thomas Aquinas said: "Anima est quodammodo omnia"[5] ("the spirit of a man is in a certain way all things"). The more that one is a person – human – the more he embraces and lives in the present instant all that has preceded and surrounds that instant.

The present is always *an action,* despite an individual's possible indolence, fatigue, and distraction. One of the truly revolutionary phrases, which announced the first stirrings of the 1968 riots, could be read on the walls of the Sorbonne in Paris: "de la présence, seulement de la présence!" This French slogan is a phrase which, when read truthfully, does not just point to the mere actuality of the instant. Rather, this word "presence" suggests all the dynamism which pulses in the instant and which derives its material from the past, and its mysterious initiative from freedom. The present is, in fact, the place, both splendid and enigmatic, of freedom, the energy which manipulates the content of the past, thereby unleashing a responsible creativity.

As we have said, in order to understand the factors which constitute him, man must start from the *present,* not the past. To begin from the past in order to come to know man's present would be a grave error in perspective. For example, if, before an inquiry into my religious experience, I stated, "Let us study the history of religions, let us analyse the primitive forms of religiosity: then we will identify the true factors of the religious experience." If I claimed to be able to use the past as a starting point like this, I could not avoid constructing a "present" image of the past itself, and running the risk of identifying the past with a conception fabricated in the present. It is only when faced with the knowledge of my present that it is possible for me to take into account my objective structure as a human being with its natural elements and dynamic, which are thus also identifiable in the past.

If I grasp *now* the factors of my experience as a human being, then I can project myself into the past and recognize the same perceptible factors in the pages of Homer, or among the Eleatic philosophers, or Plato, Virgil, or Dante. This will confirm the great unity of the human family and will really become for me an experience of civilization which grows and is enriched as time passes. Once I have used the present as a starting point to discover the values that constitute the human experience in its essential elements, then the study of the past will only illuminate ever more the way I look upon myself. But before I approach the enigma of the past, I must grasp the factors of my present personality which although unreflected upon must be clearly identifiable in experience.

A DOUBLE REALITY

In his attentive reflection upon his own experience, a person discovers in his present two types of reality: the measurable and immeasurable.

a) The first type of reality that the person finds in his or herself is quantitatively describable. It is, for example, so long or so wide, so heavy or so light. In a word, it is measurable.

Ever since I was a child in elementary school, I have been told that to measure means to compare the whole with one of its parts, used as a unit of measurement, or standard. If this is true then this also means that the whole is divisible, that the measurable can be broken down into fractions. A further, deeper characteristic fundamental to a measurable reality is the quality of divisibility. In the end, this measurable and divisible phenomenon also shows itself, under intense scrutiny, to be intrinsically and essentially mutable. For example, if I were to leave a fragment of even the hardest kind of rock on a table, and if, in a billion years or so someone were to examine it, that person would find that rock fragment to be profoundly modified. And, if I had the eye of God, I would be able to capture, within the passing instant, this infinitesimal modification in action.

This type of reality can be defined with the generic term: material. It is materiality.

b) But if a person is totally engaged in self-reflection, he will note within his "I" elements not identifiable with the measurable – these are the immeasurable and the immutable and will be defined as idea, judgment, and decision.

Let us begin with *idea* and take, for example, the idea of goodness, a criterion we find within ourselves which allows us to say of someone, "he is good." This idea cannot be measured, quantified, or modified in time. When I was an infant, I would watch my mother and would "feel" – although unreflectively – how good she was. "My mother was good," I say now, and, apart from a different, deepened consciousness, it is the very same idea of goodness which determines my affirmation now as it did then. I find that the content of my consciousness now is absolutely identical to that of my infancy – it is immutable. If, in another case, I say "this is a piece of paper," this sentence remains true forever, even in a billion centuries from now. It is a *judgment*, and, if the judgment is not false, it remains permanently true, even as, in the opposite case, it would remain permanently false. We also perceive immutablity in the phenomenon of *decision*. If I say "I am fond of this person," the definition of the relationship remains as such. Time or measure do not enter into the structural definition of the act of deciding.

Thus idea, judgment, and decision are immutable. They are neither measurable nor divisible phenomena.

It is here that this method of approach to one's human reality shows its strength, that it becomes truly evident that experience is the fount of knowledge. If the criterion by which a person assigns value to things is immanent in that person, and if the individual is not alienated from himself and is sincere, then, by observing himself in the instant of action, two kinds of elements of the self will emerge with different characteristics which evidence confirms are not reducible to one another.

To summarize: the "I" is made up of *two different realities*. To attempt to reduce the one into the other would be to deny the evidence of experience from which such a diversity emerges. These two realities may be referred to in many different ways. They have been called matter and spirit, and body and soul. Whatever the term, what is important is to understand that one is not reducible to the other.

Corollary

Now here is an observation which I consider to be highly significant. The phenomenon of death – as it enters our experience – is often associated in the Bible with a very effective expression: corruption (Ps. 16:9–10). What this word means is that in a complex unity, identified by the root *cum* (co-), quite suddenly each fragment, every part *ruit*, flees, separating from the others; or, in other words, *rumpitur*, it breaks up, it disengages itself. And this is precisely the reality of corruption. It is de-composition. This sort of vertiginous decentralization is thus applicable to that which by nature can be segmented, measured, modified. On the other hand, if there exists in me a reality which is not divisible, not measurable, and not essentially mutable, the idea of death, *as experience demonstrates*, is not applicable to me.

We must not fear this logic. We must have courage. The entire reality of the self as it appears from our experience is not completely reducible to the phenomenon of corruption. The self is not solely what one sees and what is bound to die. There is something else in the self which is non-mortal, which is immortal!

I speak of courage because human beings possess a great and readily observable weakness for which they need much support and comfort: they have an endemic fear engendered by a temptation to reduce the total image of their lives to what can be visibly and materially experienced.

THE MATERIALISTIC REDUCTION

There is a widespread objection to the existence of these two irreducible realities in a human being. This is the "materialist" objection, an objection which could easily spring forth from any one of us to the extent to which our personality is not yet the fruit of a work, which is a path towards the truth. Ultimately this objection arises from an observation that I am going to describe. Let us observe this graph.

This graph describes the trajectory of a human life in its immediately visible aspect. Human life, like all other animal life, is born of a masculine and a feminine element. In its first stages of development, it shows no describable or analysable difference from any other animal life form. The two different facets of the human being become evident only later. "You see then," the materialist would say, "those things which appear later, namely spirit, intelligence, thought, and love, spring from a material starting point. The so-called spirit then is the fruit of matter, and a human being is by nature matter."

No one can deny that, as the graph shows, there emerges in the human being an expressive level which separates itself from even the way the most evolved of animal life expresses itself. However, the materialist would argue that every expression which appears to be free from the coordinates of time and space and which thus disengages itself from the horizontal line indicating material life, originates from the same point as the others and is thus simply a sharper manifestation of the material element.

The consequences of this viewpoint are well documented. Even the most noble expressions of the human experience are rendered banal, commonplace. And the entire phenomenon of love is reduced, with bitter ease, to a biological fact.

In order to respond rationally to the materialist position, we must, first of all, point out how it contradicts experience. If, in fact, as we have seen, experience shows the existence of two types of reality, the one irreducible to the other, then I simply cannot make them coincide. If I explain the difference between the two realities by suppressing the distinction, I violate my experience: I invest it with a preconception.

Our reason urgently needs and demands unity. It is a need which is the origin of all of the fervour, all of the force of the dynamic of intelligence. But this thirst for unity cannot be emphasized to the point of deceit. It cannot force us to deny or forget one aspect so that we can explain everything else in a unified way. The German philosopher Karl Jaspers once said: "For the appearance that exists for science – the appearance we call reality – is not the reality we are. We have in our minds a technical intellect of extraordinary capacity regarding all phenomena that are accessible to research, in any definable area of research. This includes the biological and psychological phenomena of our existence. Yet there is more to us than this cognition, this know-how, this productivity."[6] Man cannot reduce himself to these processes. Moreover, Christ has already expressed this in an even more immediate and pertinent way: "Man does not live by bread alone" (Matt. 4:4).

In the second place, at the root of this forgetfulness, that is to say of this falseness (since in the name of an "a priori" it goes against the evidence of our experience), lies a methodological error. We have already seen that a human being grasps who he is only in the present instant, where there appear two irreducible factors. Now let us say that in turning my gaze back toward the past I note that, in reversing my direction, the two factors seem less visible, even to the point where I am unable to distinguish them. It is precisely this phenomenon that I will have to justify. But again, I must find an explanation which begins by affirming the two basic factors which I have discovered in this present moment.

I understand what a seed is once it has developed into a tree. Standing in front of the tree I will say, "This is a poplar tree." And, knowing what the poplar is, I will be able to analyze better the seed. This process has been repeated, so that today a botanist can say at first sight, "This is a poplar seed." What a man is can only be apparent in an actual mature development of the factors which constitute him. One understands better what a man is in Socrates or Dante than in the uneducated masses.

If I possessed a magnificent grand piano and it were possible to call in a great pianist like Arturo Bendetti Michelangeli to play it, I would be enraptured by the music which this gifted artist would be able to draw out of it. I would listen to him, focused and intense, his artistic capacity and the instrument forming one single body, one unified thing. But if someone were to sabotage this instrument before the concert, loosening all of the chords, Benedetti Michelangeli could not entertain us with his art because the instrument would not be adequate, would not meet the standards required for his musical expression.

A unity composed of two irreducible factors, where the emergence of the second is conditioned by a certain development of the first, is perfectly within our grasp, and thus rationally plausible. Thus the human body has to evolve to a certain point in order to be suitably tuned for the genial expression of the human spirit.

This conclusion values the irreducible two-fold make-up of man's nature as it manifests itself in the experience of the present, without censuring or reducing anything.

5 The Religious Sense: Its Nature

We have already outlined why, from a methodological point of view, the starting point for the kind of inquiry which interests us here is one's own experience, oneself-in-action. In addition, our initial reflections upon the matter revealed the factors in play in our experience, which have shown us the dual makeup of the human composite, the material and spiritual aspects of our lives. Now let us examine what is fundamental to the spiritual factor: the religious element.

THE LEVEL OF CERTAIN QUESTIONS

Let us draw closer to understanding the essence of this religious factor.

The religious factor represents the nature of our "I" in as much as it expresses itself in certain questions: "What is the ultimate meaning of existence?" or "Why is there pain and death, and why, in the end, is life worth living?" Or, from another point of view: "What does reality consist of and what is it made for?" Thus, the religious sense lies within the reality of our self at the level of these questions: *it coincides with the radical engagement of the self with life, an involvement which exemplifies itself in these questions.*

One of the most beautiful passages in all of literature is in Giacomo Leopardi's poem where "the nomadic shepherd in Asia" reproposes questions to a moon – which seems to dominate the infinity of earth and heaven – questions whose horizons are as infinite.

And when I gaze upon you,
Who mutely stand above the desert plains
Which heaven with its far circle but confines,
Or often, when I see you
Following step by step my flock and me,
Or watch the stars that shine there in the sky,
Musing, I say within me:
"Wherefore those many lights,
That boundless atmosphere,
And infinite calm sky? And what the meaning
Of this vast solitude? And what am I?"[1]

From the most ancient times, one of the comparisons that has been used repeatedly to identify the fragile and the ultimate enigmatic nature of human life, is leaves – dry, fallen, autumn leaves. We could say that the religious sense is the characteristic which describes nature's human level. The religious sense identifies itself with the intelligent intuition and the dramatic emotion with which a person who, upon looking at his own life and that of his fellow human beings, says: "We are like leaves ... / Away from your own branch, poor, frail leaf, where are you going?"[2] But in any case, this quotation from A.V. Arnault, which is taken up again in the themes of Leopardi, has many well-noted forerunners, and not only in Greek literature, for the theme appears in all of the literature of the world.

The religious sense is at the level of these emotions, these intelligent, dramatic emotions which are inevitable – even if the clamour and the obtuseness of our social life seem to want to stifle them:

And all combines to suppress us, partly as shame,
perhaps, and partly as inexpressible hope.[3]

AT THE CORE OF OUR BEING

These questions attach themselves to the very core of our being. They cannot be rooted out, because they constitute the stuff of what we are made. In chapter seventeen of the Acts of the Apostles in the discourse in the Areopagus, Saint Paul speaks to the Athenians about the search for the answer to the ultimate questions, questions which voice what is at the core of our being. He identifies these questions with the energy which rules over all of human mobility, continually provoking, sustaining, redefining it; this includes the movement of entire peoples, their wandering throughout the world "in search of the god," in search of the one "who gives to each one life, breath, everything" (Acts 17:25–6). Any human motion has this source, this energy at its root, and is derived from and depends upon that ultimate, original, radical, enigmatic source.

THE NEED FOR A TOTAL ANSWER

In these questions, the adjectives and the adverbs are the decisive words: *at its core*, what is the *ultimate* sense of life, *at its core*, what is reality made of? Why is it *really* worthwhile to exist, for reality itself to exist? These types of questions exhaust the energy, all of reason's searching energy. They require a total answer, an answer which covers the entire horizon of reason, exhausting completely the whole "category of possibility."

And reason, being coherent, will not give in until it has found an exhaustive answer.

> beneath the dense blue
> sky, seabirds flash by, never
> pausing, driven by images below:
> "Farther, farther!"[4]

If one's understanding of reality could be satiated solely by responding to a thousand questions, and man were to find the answer to the nine hundredth and ninety-ninth, then he would still be as restless and unsatisfied as if he were at the beginning. In the Gospel, this dimension is recalled in an interesting way: "What profit would a man show if he were to gain the whole world and lose the meaning of himself in the process? What can a man offer in exchange for his very self?" (see Matt. 16:26). This "self" is nothing more than the clamorous, indestructible, and substantial exigency to affirm the meaning of everything. And it is exactly in this way the religious sense defines the self: it is the level of nature where the meaning of everything is affirmed.

It seems right then that we should apply to the urgency of this important affirmation – indirect analogy – what Leopardi's "The Dominant Thought," says about the human feeling of love:

> mighty, belovedest
> Lord of the inmost secrets of my breast;
> Thou terrible, but dear
> Gift of the gods; companion

Unto my days of dole,
Thought, that so oft dost visit me and console.
Of thy mysterious nature
Who speaks not? Who its immemorial spell
Hath felt not? ...
How solitary becomes
This soul of mine, whene'er
Thou hast resolved to make thy dwelling there
At once all other thoughts it doth contain
Fade, as in heaven above
The flash of lightening fades. Thou, like a tower
On some deserted plain,
Standest alone, gigantic, amidst thereof.[5]

DISPROPORTION BEFORE THE TOTAL ANSWER

The more an individual is implicated in an attempt to respond to these questions, the more he perceives their power, and the more he discovers how disproportionate he is with respect to the total answer. This is the dramatic subject of Leopardi's "Thoughts":

... the inability to be satisfied by any worldly thing or so to speak, by the entire world. To consider the inestimable amplitude of space, the number of worlds, and their astonishing size, then to discover that all this is small and insignificant compared to the capacity of one's own mind; to imagine the infinite number of worlds, the infinite universe, then feel that our mind and aspirations might be even greater than such a universe; to accuse things always of being inadequate and meaningless; to suffer want, emptiness, and hence *noia* – this seems to me the chief sign of the grandeur and nobility of human nature.[6]

The inexhaustibility of the questions heightens the *contradiction* between the urgent need for an answer and our human limitations in searching for it. And still we willingly read a text inasmuch as those questions vibrate and the drama of our disproportion underlies its theme. If we are moved by the power and acuteness of Leopardi's sensitivity, it is because he evokes "the eternal mystery of our being," something that we are, an irresolvable contradiction, as the following song, "On the Portrait of a Beautiful Lady," expresses:

Learnèd consort of sounds,
By virtue of their being,
Creates for truant thought

High visions and desirings infinite:
Mysterious, the spirit of man may thus
Wander delightful seas,
As a keen swimmer goes
Among the ocean waves in his disport;
But let one false note strike
Upon the listening ear –
That moment, Paradise is turned to naught.

If, Human Nature, then,
In all things fallible
You are but dust and shade, whence these high feelings?
In any part if noble,
How is it that your worthiest thoughts and passions
Can be so lightly stirred
And roused and quenched even by such base occasions?[7]

STRUCTURAL DISPROPORTION

The inability of the answer to satisfy the constitutive needs of our self is something *structural;* in other words, it is so inherent to our nature that it represents the very characteristic of our being.

If we provisionally refer to "god" as the undefinable end point to which we are structurally referred back, then Rainer Maria Rilke's poem proclaims admirably how definitive this factor is:

Put out my eyes, and I can see you still;
slam my ears to, and I can hear you yet;
and without any feet can go to you;
and tongueless, I can conjure you at will.
Break off my arms, I shall take hold of you
and grasp you with my heart as with a hand;
arrest my heart, my brain will beat as true;
and if you set this brain of mine afire,
then on my blood I yet will carry you.[8]

Even in a million years, the issue raised by these questions will only be exasperated, unanswered.

If I, maybe, had wings
To fly above the clouds,
To number one by one the very stars,
Or wander with the storm from peak to peak,

Should I be happier then, my gentle flock?
Should I be happier, O you pale Moon?[9]

One hundred and fifty years after Leopardi, man "wanders with the storm from peak to peak," with his jets, and "numbers the stars, one by one," with his satellites. But can one say that, in the meantime, man has become even a tiny bit happier? Certainly not, because we are dealing with something which, by nature, is beyond what any human action can satisfy.

In his book, *Dalla scienza alla fede*,[10] the great mathematician, Francesco Severi, a very close friend of Einstein, proclaimed that the more he immersed himself in scientific research, the more evident it became to him that all that he discovered, as he proceeded step by step, was a function of an absolute "which set itself in opposition like an elastic barrier to its being overcome by cognitive means." The more his investigation advanced, the more the particular horizon which he approached would point beyond to yet another, thus convincing him to perceive his victory as temporary, as merely something which would then urge him on towards another x, a "something" beyond the conditions in which he operated. Whenever the research would reach a certain end point, then the object of this operation, the "x," would move further away again. The following illustration exemplifies this process: "r" is the inquisitive energy of human reason and freedom; and "x" is the temporary finish line which always points towards a further unknown.

$$r \rightarrow | \ldots x \rightarrow | \ldots x \rightarrow | \ x \ldots$$

If one attends to this dynamic seriously and with commitment, then the further an individual proceeds in an investigation, the more aware will he become of incommensurability and the disproportionate distance between the end of the investigation and the depth of the question which remains. It was a similar experience which converted Francesco Severi to religion, after – and it is he who says it – fifty years of high scientific experience. In a conversation with Einstein, a few days before the latter passed away, and which was later recounted on the feature page of a major European newspaper, Severi discussed the theme of religion with the great physicist. At a certain point, Einstein said to him, "... he who does not admit to the unfathomable mystery cannot even be a scientist."[11] Indeed, the most important characteristic of a scientist is the profound and open commitment to research, in front of any phenomenon or circumstance whatsoever. By not admitting the existence of that incommensurable "x," by not acknowledging the disproportionate gap between the ultimate horizon and human capacity, one eliminates the category of possibility, the supreme dimension of reason. This is so because only an incommensurable object can represent an unlimited invitation to the essential openness of a human being. Life is hunger, thirst, and passion for an ultimate object, which looms over the horizon, and yet always lies beyond it. When this is recognized, man becomes a tireless searcher.

Hamlet, in Shakespeare, says: "There are more things in heaven and earth, Horatio, than are dreamt of in your philosophy."[12] There will always be more things in heaven and on earth – that is in reality – than in our perception and conception of reality – that is to say in philosophy. For this reason, philosophy must possess the profound humility to be a wide open attempt, earnestly seeking adjustment, completion, and correction; it must be dominated by the category of possibility. And if this is missing, philosophy cannot advance because the next step is already predetermined by a project of those in power or a project serving one's own interests. In fact, an ideological society tends to put a freeze on every true search. Such a society uses power as an instrument to contain such research within certain limits of realization and expression. A dictatorship is never concerned that research regarding man be free research because it is the most dangerous limit to power; it is a potentially uncontrollable source of opposition.

Whenever the humble sense of human thought's essential reformability is not understood, a metamorphosis is ushered in: philosophy becomes ideology. And this metamorphosis is realized to the extent to which it can be considered "normal" to impose a certain conception of life. It is in this way that the violence of power makes its appearance.

SADNESS

Along with the conceit of power, replete with censure and denial, at the level of the single, real human being there is a corresponding great sadness, that fundamental characteristic of a life lived with awareness. St Thomas defined this sadness as "the desire for an absent good."[13]

This incommensurability of the object being sought with our own human capacity for the "conquest" of that object gives us, above all, the experience of possessing which, by its very nature, is fleeting.

... Whatever you would say or do
There is a cry within:
That is not why, that is not why!

And thus everything urges you on to
A secret question:
The act is a pretext

In God's imminence life grabs indiscriminately at failing reserves,
while everyone clings to some good as it cries out: good-bye![14]

This sadness thus rises up from the "labourious force which wearies us by keeping us in motion"; and this "weariness," which Ugo Foscolo alludes to[15] becomes, to Leopardi, "irritation," a restlessness, a sense of being unrequited, by

... a goad [that] drives me on,
And sitting there, still am I far removed
From peace or from repose:[16]

To be aware of the value of such sadness is to be conscious of the greatness of life and to intuit life's destiny. Thus Dostoyevsky was able to write about this sadness so nobly in his book *The Devils:*

[He] succeeded in touching some of the deepest chords in his little friend's heart and in evoking in him the first and still vague sensation of that eternal and sacred longing which many a chosen spirit, having once tasted and experienced it, will never afterwards exchange for some cheap feeling of satisfaction. (There are even such lovers of sensations to whom this longing is dearer than the most complete satisfaction, if such a thing were at all possible.)[17]

If sadness is a spark which is generated by the lived "potential difference" (to use an electrical term) between the ideal destination and its historical unfulfillment, if this is what sadness is, then the concealment of that "difference" – however it is done – creates the logical opposite of sadness, which is *despair:*

The mere presence of the everlasting idea of the existence of something infinitely more just and happy than I, already fills me with abiding tenderness and – glory – oh, whoever I may be and whatever I may have done! To know every moment, and to believe that somewhere there exists perfect peace and happiness for everyone and for everything, is much more important to a man than his own happiness. The whole law of human existence consists merely of making it possible for every man to bow down before what is infinitely great. If man were to be deprived of the infinitely great, he would refuse to go on living, and die of despair.[18]

It is possible that the following comment of a young woman in a letter to a friend does not, for all of that, have any less weight than that of the great Russian: "If things were only what we see, then we would be in despair." But perhaps again in no other page of literature is there more beautifully expressed the philosophical structure and everyday existential dynamism of that sadness as in the last part of "The Evening After the Holy Day of Feasting," by Leopardi:

> Alas, I hear not far along the road
> The lonely singing of a workman, coming
> Back to his poor home so late at night,
> After the sports; and fiercely my heart aches
> Thinking how all this world passes away
> And leaves no trace. For look, the festival
> Is over now, an ordinary day
> Succeeds tomorrow; all things our race has known
> Time likewise bears away. Where now is the voice
> Of the ancient peoples, the clamour of our ancestors
> Who were renowned, and that great Empire of Rome,
> The arms, and the clash they made by land and sea?
> All is silence and peace; the world is still;
> There are no tidings now remain of them.
> Once in my boyhood, when so eagerly
> We would look forward to the holiday,
> Finding it over, I lay upon my bed,
> Wakeful and very unhappy; late at night
> A singing heard along the alley ways
> Little by little dying into the distance,
> Even as this does now, gripped at my heart.[19]

THE NATURE OF THE "I" AS PROMISE

"Since what a man seeks in his pleasures is that they should be infinite and no one would ever give up hope of attaining that infinity, you see why all pleasures end in disgust. It is nature's device for tearing us away from them."[20] This observation by the writer Cesare Pavese is confirmed by other dramatic entries in his diary. When he had obtained the most highly prized Italian literary award, the Premio Strega, he commented:

You also have the gift of fertility. You are the master of yourself, of your fate. You are as famous as any man can be who does not seek to be so. Yet all that will come to an end.

This profound joy of yours, this glow of super-abundance, is made of things you did not take into account. *It was given to you.* By whom? Whom should you thank? Whom will you curse when it all disappears?[21]

And, on the day of the Premio Strega he writes: "Came back from Rome some time ago. At Rome, apotheosis. But now, this is it." However already in the first entries of his diary, we find an observation of prime value: "What a great thought it is that truly *nothing is due* to us. Has anyone ever promised us anything? Then why should we expect anything?"[22] Perhaps he did not realize that expectation is the very structure of our nature, it is the essence of our soul. It is not something calculated: it is given. For the *promise* is at the origin, from the very origin of our creation. He who has made man has also made him as "promise." *Structurally* man waits; structurally he is a beggar; structurally life is promise.

I remember the following dialogue from James Baldwin's play, *Blues for Mister Charlie:*

Richard: Did *you?* When you were young? Did you think you knew more than your mother and father? But I bet you really did, you a pretty shrewd old lady, quiet as it's kept.

Mother: No, I didn't think that. But I thought I could find *out* more, because *they* were born in slavery, but *I* was born free.

Richard: Did you find out more?

Mother: I found out what I had to find out – to take care of my husband and raise my children in the fear of God.

Richard: You know I don't believe in God, Grandmama.

Mother: You don't know what you talking about. Ain't no way possible for you not to believe in God. It ain't up to you.

Richard: Who's it up to then?

Mother: It's up to the life in you – the life in you. *That* knows where it comes from, *that* believes in God.[23]

Among my recollections from my days teaching in a high school is the memory of the tragic death of a Latin and Greek teacher: he died suddenly while teaching. At the funeral, I was off to the side as the casket was being borne away. At a certain point, I turned and saw close to me a philosophy teacher from our school who was a well-known atheist. The expression on his face was extremely tense and, without realizing it, I paused for a fraction of a second to observe him some more. Then perhaps he sensed an interrogation, for he exclaimed: "Death is the fact that lies at the origin of all philosophy."

The horizon at which a human being arrives is like a grave stone: death is the origin and the stimulus for all searching. This is so because death is the most powerful and bold contradiction in the face of the unfathomability of the human question. But this contradiction by no means removes the question. Rather, it exasperates it.

One time, I went to a sanitorium in Garbagnate, near Milan, to visit someone. As I was leaving, a nurse ran after me: a person was dying and the chaplain was nowhere to be found. The sick man was a youth, little more than twenty years old, and he was incredibly simple and pure. He impressed me by his demeanour. It seemed almost as if he were serenely counting the beats of his heart and saying, "Yet another one ..." Certain deaths are lucid like that, right up until the end. That young man died peacefully. And I reflected: If someone were to be fully aware of the death he was about to meet, would this self-awareness make the person believe that his questions were exhausted? Or would he feel them exacerbated, like the impact of running up against a wall? When an energy is highly strung, if it runs across an obstacle, it still tends to go beyond it. It does not give up.

THE RELIGIOUS SENSE AS A DIMENSION

The inexhaustible human movement searching for the ultimate depth of things – origin and destiny – that springs from the radical and implacable ardour is shaped into a stupendous image on the first page of *Joseph and his Brothers* by Thomas Mann:

Very deep is the well of the past. Should we not call it bottomless?

Bottomless indeed, if – and perhaps only if – the past we mean is the past merely of the life of mankind, that riddling essence of which our own normally unsatisfied and quite abnormally wretched existences form a part; whose mystery, of course, includes our own and is the alpha and omega of all our questions, lending burning immediacy to all we say, and significance to all our striving. For the deeper we sound, the further down into the lower world of the past we probe and press, the more do we find that the earliest foundations of humanity, its history and culture, reveal themselves unfathomable. No matter to what hazardous lengths we let out our line they still withdraw again, and further, into the depths. Again and further are the right words, for the unresearchable plays a kind of mocking game with our researching ardours; it offers apparent holds and goals, behind which, when we have gained them, new reaches of the past still open out – as happens to the coastwise voyager, who finds no end to his journey, for behind each headland of clayey dune he conquers, fresh headlands and new distances lure him on.[24]

"Mystery," says Mann, "lend[s] burning immediacy to all we say." This is the same metaphor that Cesare Pavese uses in a letter written to a woman, a professor who was participating in the production of a famous series of classical books directed by the great writer, and was translating the *Illiad* and the *Odyssey*. Pavese responds to her wish that a hint of religious urgency glimpsed in his last book, *Before the Cock Crow,* be able to develop and fulfil itself: "As to the solution which you hope for me to find, I believe that only with difficulty will I go beyond chapter fifteen in *The Cock*. In any case, it is not mistaken to feel that here is the hot point, the locus of all my consciousness."[25]

The religious sense is reason's capacity to express its own profound nature in the ultimate question; it is the "locus" of consciousness that a human being has regarding existence. Such an inevitable question is in every individual, in the way he looks at everything.

The Anglo-American philosopher, Alfred N. Whitehead, defines religion in this way: "Religion is what the individual does with his own solitariness."[26] The definition, although interesting, does not fully express the value of the intuition that gave it birth. True, this ultimate question is indeed constitutive of the individual. And in that sense, the individual is totally alone. He himself is that question, and nothing else. For, if I look at a man, a woman, a friend, a passerby, without the echo of that question resounding within me, without that thirsting for destiny which constitutes him or her, then our relationship would not be human much less loving at any level whatsoever. It would not, in fact, respect the dignity of the other, be suitable to the human dimension of the other. But that same question, in the very same instant that it defines my solitude, also establishes the root of my companionship, because this question means that I myself am constituted by something else mysterious.

So, if we wanted to complete Whitehead's definition, then yes, religion is, in fact, what the individual does with his own solitariness; but it is also where the human person discovers his essential companionship. Such companionship is, then, more original to us than our solitude. This is true in as much as my structure as question is not generated by my own will; it is given to me. Therefore, before solitude there is companionship, which embraces my solitude. Because of this, solitude is no longer true solitude, but a crying out to that hidden companionship.

A suggestive echo of all of this is to be found in the poetry of the 1951 Nobel Laureat for Literature, Pär Lagerkvist:

My friend is a stranger, someone I do not know.
A stranger far, far away.

For his sake my heart is full of disquiet
because he is not with me.
Because, perhaps, after all he does not exist?

Who are you who so fill my heart with your absence?
Who fill the entire world with your absence?[27]

CONCLUSION

Only the hypothesis of God, only the affirmation of the mystery as a reality existing beyond our capacity to fathom entirely, only this hypothesis corresponds to the human person's original structure. If it is human nature to indomitably search for an answer, if the structure of a human being is, then, this irresistible and inexhaustable question, plea – then one suppresses the question if one does not admit to the existence of an answer. But this answer cannot be anything but unfathomable. Only the existence of the mystery suits the structure of the human person, which is mendicity, insatiable begging, and what corresponds to him is neither he himself nor something he gives to himself, measures, or possesses.

The world without God would be a "tale told by an idiot, full of sound and fury, signifying nothing" (*Macbeth*, act 5, s.25, lines 26–8). So muses one of Shakespeare's characters, and the very fabric of an atheistic society has never been defined better. Life would be a "tale," a strange dream, an abstract discourse of an exasperated imagination, "told by an idiot," and, therefore, without unity. Life would be all splintered into segments, with no true order, with no vision beyond the immediate instant, "full of sound and fury," that is to say, where the single method of relationship is violence, the illusion of possession.

This long existential journey to the heart of the matter was meant to underline what the religious sense is within us – the way it emerges in our consciousness: the need for totality which is our reason, that is to say, our essential capacity for knowledge, our openness to penetrate and embrace reality to an ever greater degree.

By the very fact that a man lives, he poses this question, because this question is at the root of his consciousness of what is real, and not only does he pose the question, he also responds to it, affirming the reality of an "ultimate." For by the very fact that he lives five minutes he affirms the existence of a "something" which deep down makes living those five minutes worthwhile. This is the structural mechanism, an inevitable implication of our reason. An eye, upon opening, discovers forms and colours; so reason, by simply functioning, affirms an "ultimate," an ultimate reality in which everything subsists, an ultimate destiny and meaning. Therefore we answer those constitutive questions, either consciously and explicitly, or practically and unconsciously.

The following formula symbolizes the idea that the very existence of the question implies the existence of an answer:

$$A \to A_1$$

This formula shows A passing to A_1, and represents movement, change. An intelligent reading indicates that *a third element* – x – is involved, which, although apparently non-explicit, is contained within the formula. In fact, if you do not admit to the existence of an x, beyond A and A_1, then you would have to identify A with A_1, and, in the process, negate the "passage" from or the diversity between A and A_1 that experience makes evident. That something moves from one position to a different one means that "something else" makes this passage possible. To say that "a person becomes" or "life passes" implies the existence of *something else*. Otherwise, the statement would be a self-negating affirmation, because by not admitting that there is a hidden factor determining the passage, you end up having to concede – as has already been said – that A and A_1 are identical. And this, in turn, would negate the formula, which is a description of our experience in action.

6 Unreasonable Positions Before the Ultimate Question: Emptying the Question

PREMISE

I would now like to list, even if in a summary fashion, what I would call "unreasonable" positions which individuals assume before the questions which constitute the religious sense. They also assume these positions in answering these questions.

Now why do we use the word unreasonable? Because an unreasonable position is one which claims to explain a phenomenon, but does so in a way which does not consider adequately *all of the factors*. You simply cannot resolve a question while forgetting or denying some of the factors in play. We generalize upon this observation, and affirm that a position is erroneous whenever it neglects or negates any aspect in order to follow the dictates of its own logic. I also call these attitudes "inhuman," precisely because they are unreasonable.

Let me list six of these positions. And this is not inspired by the pure love of making lists, but because, in one way or another, these positions are either temptations, or actual attitudes all of us live. "Nihil humani a me alienum puto": I do not hold that something which has befallen another person cannot befall me.[1] Anyway, these stances define what is statistically, at least in practice, the attitude of most people.

THE THEORETICAL DENIAL OF THE QUESTIONS

First of all, the position, which I call the *theoretical denial of the questions,* defines these great questions as "senseless." According to this stance, sentences which express such questions are only grammatically correct. Otherwise, they don't make sense. They are like saying: "Look here! a donkey with wings, with a Jaguar in place of its right feet, a ballerina from the Opera instead of ears, etc." You can multiply the images as far as your fantasy wishes. But these sentences also possess another, even more serious, defect. They do not even constitute an image. They are pure words, merely sounds.

I will now recall for you the very moment when I discovered this position as a systematic attitude. I was giving a test in religion for my third-year students at the high school where I was teaching and, while the students were writing, I was walking up and down between the aisles. Having returned to the front row of desks, I picked up from one of the students the first book that caught my eye. It was one of his textbooks, *Compendium of the History of Italian Literature* by Natalino Sapegno. I began thumbing through it to pass the time, and my eye simply happened to fall upon a page where the author described the life of Leopardi. At this point, I began to read with interest, but after about half a minute I exclaimed: "Class! Stop the exam! Now you, with all of your presumptions, with all of your desire for autonomy, you read these things and accept them without question, as if you were just drinking a glass of water?" Indeed here is the text:

The questions into which one condenses the confused, indiscriminate, and reflective callow capriciousness of adolescents, their primitive and undeveloped philosophy (that is, what is life? what is the use of it? what is the purpose of the universe? and why is there pain?), those questions from which the true, adult philosopher distances himself, seeing them as absurd and lacking in any authentic speculative value and of such a nature that they bring no answer or any possibility of development, precisely these become Leopardi's obsession, the exclusive content of his philosophy.[2]

"Ah, I understand," I said to my students, "Homer, Sophocles, Virgil, Dante, Dostoyevsky, Beethoven would also be adolescents, because all of their art is driven by these questions, cries out to these needs which – as Thomas Mann used to say – give 'burning immediacy to all we say, and significance to all our striving.' I am happy to stand in the company of these men, because a man who tosses out these questions is not 'human!'"

In his *Chronicles of Contemporary Philosophy*,[3] Eugenio Garin recommends that thought be "without flights into impossible, far out things ... because the human being is the centre and master of the world ... as far as he exercises this unbound mastery in a concrete way." What kind of master of the world is he who, as the fruit of so much of his own work, generates the well-founded terror that he might destroy all of his already miserable house, "the threshing floor, whereon fierce deeds are done."[4] This "unbound mastery" means that you must think according to the mentality of the powers that be. Otherwise you will be shunned from society and, if possible, sent off to a mad house, as in Russia!

Now why are these "far out things" so impossible? Because master Garin says so? If nature has placed within me an impulse even more powerful than a rocket, a drive so deeply rooted that it actually constitutes my very self, then why must the answer to the questions generated by this impulse represent a goal so impossible that it is useless even to speak of it? Analogously John Dewey, one of the men most responsible for the pedagogy which has already formed several generations in the United States and which has arrived in Italy, after thirty years, like a rebounding wave, affirms the following:

To abandon the pursuit of reality and the search for absolute and immutable value can seem like a sacrifice. But this renunciation is the condition of entering upon a vocation of greater vitality. The search for values to be secured and shared by all, because buttressed in the foundations of social life, is a quest in which philosophy would have no rivals but collaborators among men and women of good will.[5]

To abandon the pursuit of reality, to relinquish its absolute and immutable value is too much of a sacrifice to ask of a person and could lead to suicide. According to such thinking, we ought, in fact, to forsake something towards which *nature* pushes us. And this is irrational and inhuman. It is an inadequate position.

Dewey counsels us to abandon these impossible things in order to join together and build a social life. However, this loses sight of the fact that unity among people, and thus the very possibility of a truly constructive collaboration, requires a factor which transcends the human person. And, without this, we could end up thrown together in a provisory, absolutely equivocal way, because we could never be certain of anything at all.

Even the love of a man and a woman is based on a deep bond which transcends the impulse of youth. This love is welded together by something "else," which objectifies itself in the form of a baby, a child, or, to express it more generically, a task. And, when there is this child, then what is this task? It is either consciously or obscurely, nebulously, the destiny of the child, his journey as a human person. It is this sense that brings forth and dictates the attitude of real emotion in the parents, a firm commitment, a loving feeling in all of its simplicity and totality. Without this something else which exceeds the relationship, the relationship would not last.

A relationship needs a reason, and the true reason for a relationship must tie it to the whole.

THE VOLUNTARISTIC SUBSTITUTION OF QUESTIONS

If you remove the stimulating energy of the "elementary experience," that "goad [that] drives me on," if you take away the dynamic energy which those questions determine, the motion that they give our humanity, if you empty the content of those questions which constitute precisely the essential mechanism, the motor of our personality – if you do this, then where do we find the energy to act? This energy becomes limited to a self-affirmation. Now, as the instrument of our self-affirmation is the will, or our voluntary force, it would be simply a voluntaristic energy or affirmation. It can have as its starting point: i) a taste for personal praxis; ii) a utopian sentiment; or iii) a social project. I have not listed these three categories merely by way of example: they are three fundamental forms of this position, and I can illustrate them.

i) Personal Praxis

Here is a poem by Yevtushenko:

> There are many who do not love me,
> they heap blame on me,
> and they hurl
> lightning, arrows and thunder at me.
> In a sombre and piercing way
> they laugh at my song,
> and I can feel
> their perfidious gaze upon me.
> All of this gives me pleasure.
> I am proud that these
> cannot manage to overcome me,
> to gain anything.
> With contemptuous arrogance
> I watch their brawls;
> with the joy of stone
> I deliberately prod them.
> but, known so well to all,

I go about at times with difficulty:
perplexed, tormented,
on the point of falling.
Without a false smile
I realize with anguish
that I am conceited,
that I am shrewd.
In the depths of my soul
I know that I am another.
But then why they envy me
I will never understand.
I walk silently
In the snowy street
and I ardently wish
to be conceited.[6]

Beyond his grave intuition about solitude, his outlook on life is one of voluntaristic praxis.

ii) Utopianism

Instead this voluntaristic energy is not attracted by any end recognized as an objective; rather, it almost blindly provides the goal and the end itself. Bertrand Russell, the prophet of radical culture, writes while the century is still only beginning:

The life of Man is a long march through the night, surrounded by invisible foes, tortured by weariness and pain, towards a goal that few can hope to reach, and where none may tarry long. One by one, as they march, our comrades vanish from our sight, seized by the silent orders of omnipotent Death. Very brief is the time in which we can help them, in which their happiness or misery is decided. Be it ours to shed sunshine on their path, to lighten their sorrows by the balm of sympathy, to give them the pure joy of a never-tiring affection, to strengthen failing courage, to instil faith in hours of despair.[7]

What faith? Faith in what? He is like someone who flexes his muscles, as children do when they are showing off, in order to confront time with an ideal sentiment produced by his own effort. His action is a useless hardening of the muscles of the will; he is like a sail which, although swelled by the wind, remains without a port.

Here is another typical Russell quotation, taken from *Mysticism and Logic:*

Brief and powerless is Man's life; on him and all his race the slow, sure doom falls pitiless and dark. Blind to good and evil, reckless of destruction, omnipotent matter rolls on its relentless way; for Man, condemned today to lose his dearest, tomorrow himself to pass through the gate of darkness, it remains only to cherish, ere yet the blow falls, the lofty thoughts that ennoble his little day; disdaining the coward terrors of the slave of Fate, to worship at the shrine that his own hands have built; undismayed by the empire of chance, to preserve a mind free from the wanton tyranny that rules his outward life; proudly defiant of the irresistible forces that tolerate, for a moment, his knowledge and his condemnation, to sustain alone, a weary but unyielding Atlas, the world that his own ideals have fashioned despite the trampling march of unconscious power.[8]

This passage is irrational, because, in order to write it, he had to recoil from and suffocate the needs which inspired him to write it in the first place. Such accusations mean that something objective "within" cries out and begs for more from the situation. You cannot respond to this cry with an invitation which offers no end point, an invitation where, a priori, any kind of harbour is denied.

iii) The Social Project

"Strain your muscles, puff out your cheeks. We shall realize the project of a different society!" A project made up by whom? "By me," Marx would say. "By us," others would say. This voluntaristic emphasis forgets the most acute and objective content – the personal one – which is the only place where even a social interest can originate. This position is a reduction tending towards abstraction, an impotent forgetfulness. It is not a coincidence that the philosophy produced in the USSR was almost exclusively devoted to ethics: a completely invasive moralism.

THE PRACTICAL DENIAL OF THE QUESTIONS

While the first attitude affirms that the questions make no sense, that they are without any intelligible meaning, this one, however, is purely existential, a concept which is lived: because these questions are painful, wrenching, the individual structures his life so they quite simply do not surface. The first manifestation of this attitude is well known by all, even us: "Don't think about it!" This is illustrated in Shakespeare's *Henry IV* when Dora says to Falstaff: "Thou whore son little tidy Bartholomew boar-pig, when wilt thou leave fighting o'days, and foining o'nights, and begin to patch up thine old body for heaven?"

"Peace, good Doll; speak not like a death's head; do not bid me remember mine end" (*Henry IV,* act 2, sc. 4). For most people, this is supreme wisdom.

But this same phenomenon assumes a different and surprising shape, for example, in Kazimierz Brandys' "The Defense of Granada"; the society creates diversions in order to obscure the great interest which is the essential question, the question of meaning. And it is unable to succeed, so life in society is supplanted by alcohol (or today, by drugs).

In the streets of our city the crowd moves along the widened sidewalks under buildings taller than they have ever been. In a deaf and sorrowful disquietude, it seeks out the flavour of the present day. Thirsty for strong excitations, it turns to the cinema, the stadiums, the taverns. The crowd is unsatisfied by the social motivation for existence, even though it ought to recognize the logic, pointed out every day with a thousand arguments. Generally these arguments are convincing: the crowd is not made up of madmen: it has understood the importance of work in life, it takes seriously organized effort, it feels respect for material energy, the source of future successes. All this, however, does not disperse its uneasiness. The principles and the goals do not appease its yearnings. Tormented by a confused desire, longing to forget the program for its realization, the crowd wants to discover the flavor of life, which allows it to taste the pleasure of the space of existence. The crowd is not exacting in all of this, it takes that which is given it. Alcohol contains the most secure guarantee of reconciling one's self with the present, a half-liter bottle contains the desired percentage of irrational ...[9]

In Shakespeare's *Tempest,* at a certain point, Antonio states: "The latter end of his commonwealth forgets the beginning" (act 2, sc. 1, line 154). Gonzalo continues to dream about a just society which might be built. This could be an ultimate goal. Where is the error of today's society? It forgets the beginning which is in the conscience of human beings, who cry out these ultimate questions. And these questions penetrate our relationships with our children, friends, strangers; they permeate our work and daily lives, the way we speak – "What a beautiful day it is!" – and our confrontation with social problems. In fact, individuals are attracted to the social question not because of its internal logic, but precisely due to a passion or thirst for justice which will never find complete and exhaustive measures or yardsticks, ever.

In the initial phases of the beat generation, one of the most well-known slogans was this: "Gotta go. Gotta go. Don't know where, but we gotta go." Doing, in order not to feel, not to deepen an otherwise obvious restlessness. Such a sceptical tone underlies this attitude which supports most people's irresponsibility, because scepticism always coincides with the flight from an involvement with a total reality in all of its integral dimensions. An apocryphal book of the Bible, the fourth chapter of Ezra, asks: "What good is it that there is the promise of undying hope if we are tossed here into unhappiness?"[10] "Therefore," one could conclude, "let us relinquish those ultimate questions and get busy with being happy here!"

But the most noble standpoint, the one most well formed and philosophically motivated, and the only dignified alternative to an involvement proper to a sincerely religious life, that is to say, a life truly committed to the essential questions, is the stoic ideal of perfect emotional imperturbability. John Falstaff devoted himself to swordplay, others to alcohol or drugs, or even the drug of scepticism. But there remains a position much more complex and cunning and it sounds like this: "It is impossible to answer these questions; therefore we must anaesthetize ourselves." Here the dignified and sage person has become the master of himself and constructs, imagines and realizes a totally self-proclaimed and rational equilibrium. And come what may, this equilibrium renders him firm and fearless. No matter what philosophy sustains the conception of the person, as long as it is irreligious, this will be its supreme ideal.

In this poem by Yevtushenko, we can see, above all, an example of this imperturbability as it is practically lived and aesthetically felt:

In over-crowded trams
all packed in together,
swaying together,
together we stagger. All made equal
by an equal weariness.
From time to time we are swallowed
by the subway,
and then the subway spits us forth again from
its smoking mouth.
Through unknown streets, between white eddies
we ride, men beside men.
The breath of each of us mingles,
our footprints are changed and confused.
From our pockets we pull our tobacco.
We whine some latest song.
Knocking each other with our elbows,
we say "excuse me" – or we say nothing,
The snow strikes tranquil faces.

We exchange mean, deaf words.
It is just us, all of us, us here,
we are all together
what abroad they call Moscow!
We who here go about with our bags
under our arms, with our parcels and bundles,
it is us who launch space ships to the heavens
and perplex hearts and brains.
Each one on his own, through
his own Sadovye, Lebiazie, Trubnye,
on his own schedule
without knowing each other
we, brushing against each other,
on we go ...[11]

Impermeability, total aridity.

But this is the ideal of so much contemporary literature. I would like to invite you to read the ending of *A Farewell to Arms*[12] by Ernest Hemingway: Frederic Henry overcomes the pain of the death of Catherine by turning his back and walking off – this is the "rational" man, the master of himself!

In the column "Italy Asks" in the weekly newsmagazine, *Epoca,* Augusto Guerriero reprinted the following request of one of his readers:

I turn to you as the only one who can help me. In 1941, at only seventeen years of age, I took seriously a fascist slogan calling us to arms and left my house and my studies, signing up for the "M." Battalion. I fought in Greece against the partisans. I was wounded, then captured by the Germans and, as a prisoner, removed to Germany. During my imprisonment I contracted tuberculosis. Returning from prison I hid my illness from everyone, even my family. And this because, in the mean, common mentality, someone sick with TB, even though it is not contagious (as it was in my case), is a person to be avoided, to pity and to approach only if forced and then only by taking a thousand precautions. And I wanted none of that. I knew I was not dangerous and wanted to live like all other men, together with all other men.

I took up my studies again, got a degree and found some work. I have lived thoughtlessly for years, forgetting that I had ever been ill. Now, however, this sickness is progressing, and I feel that I am dragging myself toward the end. From day to day, I distract myself, seeking to live intensely. But at night I can't get to sleep, and the thought that in a little while I will no longer exist makes me break out in a cold sweat. Every so often I think I'll go crazy. If I had faith I would be able to take refuge in that, I would find the necessary resignation. But, unfortunately, I lost my faith a long time ago. And the many, perhaps too many, books that I've read that made me lose it haven't given me in exchange that coldness, that tranquility that permits others to face this step serenely. I've ended up stripped and disarmed once and for all. And this is why I turn to you. I admire your serenity, which is transparent in all of your writings, and I envy you this serenity. I am sure that a letter of yours would be a great relief for me and would make me stronger. I ask you please to help me.

Guerriero replied:

But tell me: What can I do for you? Write you a letter? And what good would writing you a letter do? I only write about politics and what use would it be to write to you about politics: You need for someone to talk to you about other things, and I never write about those things, in fact I never think about them, and it is precisely not to think about them that I write about politics and about other things that, in the end, don't mean a thing to me. In this way I manage to forget myself and my misery. This is the problem: to find the way to forget ourselves and our own misery.

It is not wise to affirm: "by day I distract myself, seeking to live intensely," for any advice which counsels us to forget cannot be wise. Does trying to forget assure that one lives intensely, like a man, reasonably? These positions do not do us justice.

This ideal of imperturbability, even when reached through an implacable mastery of the self – besides being inadequate and illusory, due to the fact that it does not last – is also at the mercy of chance. Yes, you can train yourself to be imperturbable and unassailable. But to the extent that you are not arid, are intensely human, sooner or later your construction, perhaps the fruit of an ascetic work of many years, a work of relentless philosophic reflection and presumption, will still need only a puff of wind to make it crumble.

One of the youthful short stories of Thomas Mann vividly demonstrated this to me. The great genius truly captures the dominant culture, but it is impossible for him not to let the remaining inquietude in and the ultimate failure of this culture seep through to the surface. The title of that story was *Little Herr Friedmann*.[13]

The protagonist was the fourth son of a rich and noble family in a certain German city. An accident had befallen him shortly after birth and had left him crippled, with a protruding chest and a hunched back, his head sunken in. His body was seriously deformed. Consequently, he developed an extraordinary self-defense mechanism: this individual instinctively and unconsciously applied all of his intelligence and force of will to construct a "modus vivendi," a way of life undisturbed by instinct, attractions, and proposals. He understood by sheer intuition that he could not permit himself what would be allowed other men. Thus he learned to live under strict limitations. He grew up in this monotonous way, with one kind of order: total equilibrium. The people of the city admired him because they understood that he was a man who controlled himself with intelligence, although they did not love him. There was, however, just one single hobby to which he was dedicated. This was, so to speak, the theatre. Symbolically, he was never an actor in life, but a spectator. The ideal of this position of imperturbability, in fact, is to live as much as possible, as a spectator of the equivocal and dangerous fervour of life on the stage. But an absolutely unforseeable and out of place experience destroyed this perfect order – he fell in love and this equilibrium was destroyed in a few days, indeed, in a mere moment. And all of the energy which had gone into this self control, all of the intelligence and the force with which it had been constructed, all this collapsed with a single blow and reduced him to the cold act of suicide.

The answer to the questions of life does not lie in this dominion, this self-control.

The crickets, which fall quiet for an instant at the splash of little Herr Friedmann as he drowns himself, bring to mind the indifference of the "silvery donkey" in Giosuè Carducci's "Before Saint Guido," A.J. Cronin's *The Stars Look Down,* or Giovanni Pascoli's poem "The Book":[14] the crickets, the stars, the ass, all symbolize nature, arid and insensitive nature, which abandons man in complete solitude when man allows himself to fall away from the impulse toward mystery, toward which the constitutive questions of his heart authoritatively drive him.

And the "hushed laughter" of people along the street betrays an estrangement from and an imperviousness to the tragic thirst for love and happiness in the heart of little Herr Friedmann, exactly like the unconscious indifference of the crickets.

7 Unreasonable Positions Before the Ultimate Question: Reduction of the Question

The first three positions we have listed – the theoretical denial, voluntaristic substitution with one's own emotional ideals and the practical – are analogous to each other in that they all attempt to empty the questions of their content. The next three positions also have a common denominator: to one degree or another they take seriously the reality of the constitutive stimulus of reason, but they reduce it: the first one stops in midstride, the second self-destructs because of the difficulty of the answer, while the third – which is the most deceitful and cynical – turns these sacred questions, in which lies our very life, into an instrument of power.

THE AESTHETIC OR SENTIMENTAL EVASION

In this position, although the person accepts the questions, measures and calibrates them with feeling, he does so without self-involvement, without committing his own freedom. Rather, the individual finds enjoyment in expressing the emotions stimulated by the questions. The search for life's meaning, the urgency, the need for life to have a meaning becomes a spectacle of beauty: it assumes an aesthetic form.

Nikos Kazantzakis, the greatest modern Greek poet, says at a certain point in *The Odyssey:* "Freedom, my lad, is neither wine nor a sweet maid, not goods stacked in vast cellars, no nor sons in cradles; it's but a scornful, lonely song the wind has taken."[1] Here we see how the value of freedom is tied to the total meaning. But the poet does not venture beyond this point, this single expression of an aesthetic motion.

The next poem to come to mind is "Jaufré Rudel" by Giosuè Carducci:

> Lady, what is this life of ours?
> The fleeting shadow of a dream. *THE SHADOW OF A FLEETING DREAM*
> Now end the fable's transient hours,
> 'Tis only love that knows not death.[2]
> *IT IS*

PUNTO DI APPOGGIO The existential seriousness of these human questions cannot find a foothold in the frivolous aestheticism of these questions' echoes.

For another example, let us say that while sailing in the Mediterranean towards Gibraltar, I encountered a spectacle of dolphins performing their acrobatics, swimming after one another, synchronized and in perfect form. Even if I did see this, still I am not able to assert along with André Gide, a witness to an analogous scene, that aesthetic taste is what makes life worth living – nature as a continuous flow of aesthetic pleasure. This viewpoint cannot satisfy a mother whose son is dying, nor an individual out of work. While the urgency we feel opens out on to life in all its concreteness and completeness, we cannot stop in midstride to pamper ourselves with an emotional experience, which becomes only evasion and waste.[3] *SPACE*

Despite everything, it seems to me that this beautiful poem by Yevtushenko displays this same detached aestheticism:

> After every lesson, in a thousand ways
> everyone comes to you, they interrupt you.
> From children's mouths you hear
> compliments full of sweet praise.
> There are many good things
> in this life: Appointments
> flowers, the theater ..., all that's missing is
> what you desire – you lack,
>   the essential thing
> And here, you run up the stairs,
> You are eighteen years old.
> In your satchel
>   you have, with your Leninine profile,
> your membership card of the komsmol.
> In the usual tick-tock of midnight
> asleep in your apartment
> you ask yourself
>   – I know –
> the help of some severe idea,
> and you think of the revolution,

TO UNDO , UNDID , UNDONE —
DISFARE , SCIOGLIERE —

or you look for great love,
as you undo your pig-tails   TRECCE   FOLTE
    sciogli
                    of shining
brown hair.
In your house there is only this slow ticking of the pendulum.
This dialogue of yours with your soul
you are still truly very young.
I am old compared with you, really,
                              old.
You are my young traveling companion
I, your old companion.
I am assailed by the thought of what will happen to your brown hair
and if I torment you with the disquieting
search for something greater, something sublime,
I, who was the first to believe in many things,
have believed so that now you also can believe ...[4]

Evasion and waste: these are well-known characteristics of many relationships, at least at the beginning. "'Tis far off; and rather like a
dream than an assurance that my remembrance warrants," says Mi-
randa in *The Tempest* (act 1, sc. 2, lines 44–6). The dream takes its cue SPUNTO
from something true, has an ideal impulse which creates a certain DATO
imaginative, emotive halo. But it is without a "base," a given foundation, which must be continually regained so that we can, by obeying
it, verify it with ever-increasing certainty!

THE DESPERATE NEGATION

Of all the erroneous attitudes, this is the most dramatic, the most
impassioned, and the most serious. This position totally denies that
an answer to the question exists. And the more one feels the urgency
of these questions, the more pronounced is the denial. In the preceding stances, the individual sought to destroy the questions – but here, POSIZIONI
no. Here they are taken seriously. The individual is too serious to
deny them. But, at a certain point, the difficulty of the answers causes
the person to say: "it is not possible."

This position is the most dramatic because here man's pure option
– between yes and no – is played out. But between these two choices,
which one corresponds more to the origin, to *all the factors* of our
structure? That is to say, which is *more* reasonable? This is the point.
Authentic religiosity is the defense, to one's last breath, of reason, of
human conscience. Rationalism often destroys the very possibility of
reason, of reason as a category of possibility.

TO PLAY OUT :   GIOCARE UN AZZARDO DI
            IL RAMO

I want to take inspiration from a quotation from *Minima Moralia*[5] by T. Adorno, the great thinker of the Frankfurt School. In the morning when your alarm rings and you have to get up, a voice in your head says: "Stay here." You would not be living up to yourself to remain there in bed. Thus it is, observes Adorno, "when we hope in salvation, a voice in our head says that the hope is vain." But we would not be living up to our selves if we gave credence to this voice, because it does not provide a reason why the hope still persists. Indeed, continues Adorno, "it is this, this alone, impotent hope" which allows us to breathe, that is to live. For this reason, he speaks of the "ambivalence of sadness," affirming the sadness of opting for a contradiction. All self-reflection, he asserts, "cannot do more than patiently redraw *RI DISEGNARE* new approaches to and images of the ambivalence of sadness: the truth is not separable from the obsession that salvation emerge from the images of appearance, without appearing." The mental and psychological choice which Adorno describes – that is, the affirmation that there is no salvation – is not separable from the "obsession that salvation emerge from the figures of appearance." The true aspect of Adorno's position lies in his latter observation. What Adorno calls "obsession" is the structure of the human being, it is what we call "heart," or elementary experience: to negate it is to deny the existence of something that is real. It is unreasonable, inhuman.

Cesare Pavese discusses the same sadness in a calmer way: "Has anyone ever promised us anything? Then why should we expect anything?"[6] Here is the obsession: it is the structure of our life, that is promise, as we have already seen; the inevitability of the profound questions is the emergence of the promise. To forget or deny is to be irrational.

The despair born of such a denial is documented in a fascinating *ESPRIMERE* way by those who know how to depict the human drama. I will illustrate this in the following three different representations: a) the impossible aspiration; b) reality as illusion; and c) nothingness as *NULLA* *COME* essence. *ESSENZA*

a) The Impossible Aspiration ("The Impotent Hope")

BRAVO

The following quotation is taken from a novel by Jack Kerouac.

... see my hand uptipped, learn the secret of my heart, give me the thing, give me your hand, take me to the safe place, be kind, be nice, smile; I'm too tired now of everything else, I've had enough, I give up, I quit, I want to go home, take me home O brother in the night, take me home, lock me in safe – take me to where there is no home, all is peace and amity, to the place that

I GIVE UP : ABBANDONARE CEDERE

never should have been or known about, to the family of life – My mother, my father, my sister, my wife and you my brother and you my friend – take me to the family which is not – but no hope, no hope, no hope, I wake up and I'd give a million dollars to be in my bed.[7]

This "no hope, no hope" is evidently an option, a choice, suggested, certainly, by painful experience: but this negation does not cover, or give a reason for all of the factors in play. What I have called "the impossible aspiration" then is not so much an openly negative option as it is like stopping oneself, bewildered, on the threshold of the true conclusion – it is like being the prisoner of a query which continually reopens the original wound. We have already quoted from the song of Leopardi, 'On the Portrait of a Beautiful Lady," and it is the dramatic conclusion of this realistic and fascinating evocation which interests us here: "everlasting mystery of our being!" exclaims the poet.[8] This is the question, this is the true threshold of the conclusion. Leopardi's assertion that an answer is not possible, paradoxically becomes a positive testimony: the negation emerges so evidently from the outside and is so clearly extraneous to the powerful evocation of the entire human heart that the "no" appears as an evidently unjust choice.

b) Reality as Illusion

I will explain this position with an exceedingly beautiful poem by Eugenio Montale.

> Perhaps some morning, walking in a vitreous, clear
> air, turning I shall see the miracle appear,
> the nothingness around my shoulders and the void
> behind, and know the terror of the drunken paranoid.
>
> Then suddenly, as on a screen, confusion
> of hills, and houses, planted in the usual illusion.
> But it will be too late, and I shall be warier
> as I move among those men who do not turn, with my secret terror.[9]

Never have I found reality's contingent nature so well described, the perception that reality does not make itself. What is most evident to a true adult is that he or she does not make him or herself: and the human being, as I have already asserted, is that level of nature where nature becomes conscious of itself, aware that it does not subsist by itself, that things do not subsist in themselves. This experience is also, for the individual, the threshold of a discovery, of the fact of creation – the realization that things are made by an Other. Faced then, with Montale's "void behind" me, we confront two hypotheses: either things are not made by themselves, and are created by an Other, or else they are illusions and are nothing. We must decide: which of the two hypotheses corresponds better to reality as it appears to our experience, and not just to one of our opinions, perhaps deduced from a current ideology? Undoubtedly the hypothesis that reality is made by an Other is the valid one because it does coincide with our experience: even if reality is ephemeral and insubstantial, nonetheless it is. Montale, from this vertiginous (like a "drunken paranoid") perception of the insubstantial and ephemeral appearance of things does not reach that reasonable recognition which is the origin of every true religious experience and authentic prayer. Instead, he detaches himself from the impulse which shows him that things exist, denies the evident fact that they do exist, and abandons himself to a desperate negation. Thus, in the poem, we see him choose the "no": and "no" is a sad and tragic option.

c) Nothingness as Essence

Montale's poem catches man in the dizzying moment in which he chooses the abyss. The following poem, by Cesare Pavese, describes the reality of that abyss.

> You are like land
> that no one has ever talked of.
> You expect nothing,
> only words
> flowing out from the depths
> like fruit among the branches.
> A wind reaches you.
> Dry, twice-dead things
> obstruct you and blow away with the wind.
> Ancient limbs and words.
> You quiver in summer-time.[10]

Immediately, the option is negative: "You are like a land that no one has ever talked of." Because "you are," you depend upon something Ultimate, and in order to negate this Ultimate, you must deny this "You" – "You" being the word which emerges most naturally from the very depths of your origins. Moreover, it is the same as denying nature to say "you expect nothing." Thus, there exists for you no living thing. "Dry, twice-dead things," neither leaves with branch nor branch with trunk, follows the biblical idea from the psalm, according to which everything for man without God is *dust*, every grain is purely haphazardly tossed in with another, with no connection. "Ancient limbs and words:" not a body, not a discourse – rather all arrives from a preceding whirling vortex, without meaning. And here is the contradiction which grinds down everything, the uninterrupted turbine of the abyss: "you quiver in summertime." Summer is hot, and you are cold. You shiver, you are unable to act, to construct. The only warmth, in fact, which allows the individual to render the past a construction in the present is the recognition of a fullness of intelligence and love, of "meaning" in those "depths from which you flow," as the total outlook of human consciousness demands.

ALIENATION

Although this final position asserts that life has an entirely positive meaning, it denies that it is valuable or true for the person.

This position would have the ideal of life reside in a hypothetical evolution in a future, an evolution in which all should collaborate as the only reason for living, and where the spiritual dynamic of the individual and the evolving mechanism of social reality will be finalized. This phenomenon, in its entirety, is described by that supremely equivocal word: *progress*. This slant on reality considers the fundamental questions of the human being as mere functional stimuli, useful for the edification of progress almost similar to some kind of deceitful trick which nature plays in order to force us into serving its irreversible project.

But there is a radical objection to be made here. The fundamental questions signal, within the very nature of man's *personal* dimension, the emergence of the irreducible originality of his *personality*. Those questions constitute my personhood. They are identified with my very reason and consciousness. They are the essence of my self-awareness and their resolution has to touch me, it directly concerns *me*. An answer to those questions is not given, unless it is given to *me*, for *me*.

It is impossible to make the fulfilment of a collectivity in some hypothetical future the answer to those questions without dissolving man's identity or alienating the human being within an image which frustrates and ignores the deep complex of the "I"s urgent needs. This profound complex constitutes my "I," even as diverse tissues form my body: to deny this would be like dissolving the irreducible identity of my body. The questions *are* my "*I*." In the progressivist solution, however, the "I" has no answer – it is alienated. This is an unreasonable explanation, inadequate to all of the factors in play. The "I" would have to destroy itself in order to realize this type of reality. To eliminate this principal and fundamental factor, which is the "I," to dissolve it does not resolve the question. This would be to dispose of the most inconvenient and yet decisive factor. I leave it to Dostoevsky in *The Brothers Karamazov* to restate this rational evidence:

Oh, all that my pitiful earthly Euclidean mind can grasp is that suffering exists, that no one is to blame, that effect follows cause, simply and directly, that everything flows and finds its level – but, then this is only Euclidean nonsense. I know that and I refuse to live by it! What do I care that no one is to blame, that effect follows cause simply and directly and that I know it – I must have retribution or I shall destroy myself. And retribution not some-where in the infinity of space and time, but here on earth, and so that I could see it myself. I was a believer, and I want to see for myself. And if I'm dead by that time, let them resurrect me, for if it all happens without me, it will be too unfair. Surely the reason for my suffering was not that I as well as my evil deeds and sufferings may serve as manure for some future harmony for someone else. I want to see with my own eyes the lion lie down with the lamb and the murdered man rise up and embrace his murderer. I want to be there when everyone suddenly finds out what it has all been for.[11]

This position is reasonable, because it takes into account all of the factors of the situation, even if the way in which the solution is reached is beyond comprehension and adequate images. It is reason-able because here we are discussing an event which overcomes the limits of our existential experience, of the now.

I would now like to underline two observations.

1. There is a profound and original nexus between the fulfilment of my person, my path as a person and the destiny of the world, that is to say, the incremental increase of the cosmos, the passage of the human race towards its ultimate design. This is a great truth, af-firmed, above all, in the Christian idea of *merit*. According to this con-cept, the individual begins to live up to and grow towards his destiny in the measure in which his action "moves," is *for* the world, builds up the world and humanity. It does so if it is "offered" to God, carried out for God's total design for the world. "Is the object of life only to live? Will the feet of God's children be fastened to this wretched earth? It is not to live, but to die, and not to hew the cross, but to mount upon it, and to give all that we have, laughing! There is joy, there is freedom, there is grace, there is eternal youth!" So muses Anne Vercors in front of the body of his daughter Violaine in Paul Claudel's drama, *The Tidings Brought to Mary*. "What is the worth of

the world compared to life? And what is the worth of life if not to be given?"[12] On the other hand, Diderot's position, straight from the Enlightenment, as expressed in the *Encyclopedia*, is such an inhuman abstraction:

O Posterity, holy and sacred! the sustainer of the oppressed and of the unhappy, you who are just, you who are incorruptible, you who will reveal the good man and unmask the hypocrite, idea consoling and certain, abandon me not. Posterity is for the philosopher what the other world is for the religious.[13]

This seems to me to be a return to the most primitive state one can possibly imagine. It is like when God, in order to explain to Abraham that He would favour him, promised him a long line of descendants. But we are far away from that time. Nonetheless, this represents the same mentality. Today, with less colourful words, we hear it said to us that the point of all our energy is to dissolve ourselves into the progress of the future!

2. This progress towards the future, in whose hands is it? The powerful, those who have the force and circumstances others do not. Those rich, who perhaps no longer rise to the top by the sweat of their own brow, but are born with a certain shrewdness for the political life or the use of an inheritance. And also this is an alienation, and an ignoble loss of the "I."

It is the rebellion against this kind of alienation that has lent such great nobility to the Russian spiritual revival of the 1970s and 1980s, despite the constant risks of persecuted secrecy and harassment by those seeking to dissolve it. The following poem is indicative of one poet's rebellious thrust.

> I curse all this pseudo-progress,
> My throat is sore from technical terms;
> Having given them voice and soul,
> I'll be damned for the fact a woman will,
> Bolting down her food capsules,
> One day in the future, ask someone:
> "In Volume 3 of Voznesensky,
> What is that creature, the cyclotron?"
>
> I answer: "Its bones have rusted away;
> It's no more scary than a troika racing by:
> Technologies and states live for a day,
> Then go their way, and pass us by."

Only one thing on earth is constant
Like the light of a star that has gone;
It is the continuing radiance
They used to call "the human soul."[14]

Churchill, when he was called to America for a triumphal tour as the saviour of civilization, also visited the Massachusetts Institute of Technology (MIT). The dean of humanities gave a grand speech in which he exalted the definitive value of this civilization of man, now arriving at its ultimate goal: to dominate the human being, as it has already dominated everything else – to be able to program thoughts, feelings. In this way, a new Hitler could never be born. Churchill stood up and replied, and I quote: "I shall be very content, personally, if my task in this world is done before that happens."[15] The politics of today are governed by this type of culture all over the world. It is for this reason that there must be a revolution for the defense of what is human, and this revolution can only come about under the banner of religiosity. It must be authentically religious, and therefore, with authentic Christians in the front lines.

After analyzing these positions, I must make the crucial point of our critical denunciation: these positions which we have described do not entirely correspond to all of the factors which experience shows to us to be in play. They are dreams, unmindful of what precedes them, of the starting point; they are errors in which a tension or passion for an end-point, creates a disregard for the original data, and this leads to madness. All of them possess a correct aspect, or a plausible pretext which, however, is given disproportionate weight.

Dostoevsky asserts the most evident truth when he writes that the bee knows the secret of its beehive, the ant knows the secret of its anthill, but man does not know his own secret – the structure of a human being is a free relationship with the infinite, and therefore, it has no limits. It bursts through the walls of any place within which one would want to restrain it.[16]

The questions and the constitutive evidence of the "heart" (or of the "elementary experience") are the existential outlines of the free relationship with the infinite.

8 Consequences of the Unreasonable Positions Before the Ultimate Question

The six categories we have discussed all devalue the questions which we have recognized as expressing the human being's specific originality. They strip them of their substance and weight. The concomitant loss of meaning carries with it grave cultural consequences. The individual loses control of himself, of all of the factors which constitute him. He becomes like a driver who loses control of his car, and the movement of the car takes over the driver, or better yet, sets itself on a course without direction, wide open to any collision.

The following are the consequences of these positions: first, an individual breaks with the past; second is solitude; and third involves the elimination of one's own freedom as an anthropological and social characteristic.

THE BREAK WITH THE PAST

The loss of meaning tends to annul the individual's personality, which acquires density and weight precisely as need, intuition, perception, and the affirmation of meaning. Let me explain myself.

A dog will rub itself against a car without grasping the car's meaning, that is to say, its aim and use. In the same way, a person could also play around with a car without being able to use it, "possess" it. He would not be able to "possess" the car, in as much as he had not grasped its meaning. It would remain extraneous to him. In such a circumstance, the human being is paralyzed, neither capable of understanding nor utilizing anything. This loss of meaning reduces the personality and induces a type of depression that blurs the individual's sense of the past.

I would like to explain this by taking up another analogy. Without knowing the meaning of an instrument placed before you, how could you handle it? You manipulate it as a baby would. You play with it. But what do we signify when we say "to play" with an object? We mean that the connection between the person and the object is determined by an end not adequate to the object itself (unless, obviously, that object has been created for play); the connection is not intelligent or in order, controlled or directed. For example, a baby's relationship with a camera he plays with would be based upon pure reactivity; he would be struck by the glint of light on its lens, and, being able to see himself with it, he would be attracted by the enigma of what lies within the box. Consequently, he sticks his hand inside, breaking it to bits and pulling out all of the little pieces. It is not very different for a person who has lost the meaning of his or her life, the answer to those questions. You cannot say that this person is merely playing around with the world, because the situation is simply too dramatic and tragic for that – the term "to play around" would apply only in some cases and in certain moments. However, we can use the word already cited, "he reacts." The human person reacts. The criteria for his or her bond with reality is reactivity, reaction.

Reactivity as the criterion for a relationship with reality burns the bridges linking us to the richness of history and tradition, that is to say, it cuts us off from the past. Reactivity signifies the absence of an all-encompassing, recognized, pursued, and desired meaning, a refusal to respect all of the implicated factors. Since it is not ordered toward the overall meaning of events, when reactivity takes over, the first thing it produces is a break with the past. Reactivity blocks the link with history, burns the bridges with everything that has converged to form this moment. I would like to refer here to a passage from Chinese knightly literature from between the eighth and ninth centuries, which could just as well have been written today.

> Certainly there were many evils that
> the men of ancient times suffered.
> But there were, however, the men of wisdom.
> These would teach [to other men] the principle
> of mutual cohabitation and of mutual support.
> These wise ones chose their rulers and teachers.
> They put to flight the reptiles, serpents and wild beasts,
> and they established man's [primacy].

For those who were cold, they made clothes;
for those who were hungry, they prepared food;
for those who lived in trees ... or in caves ... they made houses.
They instructed the workers that they [might make] utensils;
the merchants that they might trade things
that they had or of which they were lacking;
the doctors who would use the medicines ...
[They inculcated] recognition toward benefactors;
[they instituted] norms that would assign each to his proper place.
[They created] music that would dissipate the sadness built up in the heart,
the government that would give a shock to negligence,
the punishments that would break down obstinance.
And since men were cheating one another
the wise ones dictated to them ...
bushels, litres, weights and scales in order that they keep faith in selling.
...

And now there are those who say
"... let's smash these bushels, let's smash these scales
and then the people won't have anything to argue about anymore."

The ancient ones, wishing to make manifest the force of intelligence,
first governed their State; but in order to govern their State,
first they organized their families;
but in order to organize their families,
were first mindful of their conduct;
but in order to mind their conduct,
first they made straight their hearts,
but to make straight their hearts,
first they rectified their intentions ...
The principles [of the ancient law] were understood easily and put ... into practice ...

Today [however] they want to exalt the laws of barbarians,
indeed they want to prefer them to those [ancient ones] ...
Today those who claim to [innovate] reject the State and the family
and abolish natural relations, in such a way
that the son no longer respects the father,
the subject no longer submits [to the law] ...

So then what should be done?
It is necessary that men act like

true men ... and that they be [newly]
instructed in the [ancient] doctrine ...
Let us hope that this be so.[1]

Today this destruction of the past has the audacity to present itself as an ideal. It is a generalized alienation.

But there is another consequence. If the sense of the past is blurred and the present turns to pure reaction, then the fecundity of the future also dries up because, quite simply, we construct the future with the present. In fact, this moment, this instant is replete with energies, images, riches, and abundance of feelings: materials for constructing the future. Where do they come from? How shallow is an action born of a pure reaction in the instant! And indeed, ultimately, we cannot even conceive of this. We must recognize that – in order to react *now* – we need to use something given to us in the past: flesh, bones, intelligence, heart. Therefore, although the force for building the future lies within the energy, the imaginativeness, the courage of the present, the richness of the present comes from the past.

The present, then, is that mysterious moment where the richness of the past is conceived and reconceived in an image not only provoked and made possible by the past, but also filtered through the mystery of the originality of my present, as we have already stated, my freedom, which is always played out in the present. But the content and the richness are in the past. The more powerful one's personality, the more one will be able to recover all of the past; and the more childish an individual, the more he or she forgets about what has gone before, and is unable to use it, even when reminded of it.

A writer of the *Samizdat*, that is, underground Soviet literature, says: "We well know that the lie of all revolutions is in the fact that they are strong and concrete in condemning and in destroying, but are absolutely weak and abstract in building and creating."[2] In other words, they are impotent before the future, because, by burning all of their bridges with the past, they have refused to see the past as the cohesive tissue of that very present which they hold so dear. Because even as the human person is one, so too is history, and the force of the present undertaking lies in all that has preceded it.

INCOMMUNICATIVENESS AND SOLITUDE

Incommunicativeness. But this blurring of the sense of the past, which dries up the fecundity of the future, also reduces all human dialogue and communication to a vortex. Indeed, the past is the humus in which the dialogue is rooted.

This is one of the fundamental concepts of Alexander Solzhenit-syn, which he expresses in a fascinating way when he speaks of the Russians as a people whose memory has been amputated. Now, an individual whose memory has been amputated is sad, impoverished, diminished, dried up. So what is more of a passionate and communicative expression of my personality than my remembrance of the past? It is precisely there, in the memory of the past, that my commitment to the present and my responsibility for the future find footholds, inspirations, paradigms, support, and evidence. The memory of the people is reduced to pieces. "Whole speechless generations are born and die off who do not tell each other about themselves," because they are prevented from remembering, says the Russian writer.[3] These are notes which strike like a sword at the roots of today's mortal infirmity.

Communication, dialogue, from where do they arise? From what? They spring from experience, whose depth lies in the capacity of memory: the more charged I am with experience, so too the more I am able to speak and communicate with you, and the more I find connections in your position – no matter how arid it may be – to what is within myself. Human dialogue and communication are rooted in experience. Indeed, where does the aridity, the flacidity of shared living, of the shared life in the community, come from if not from the fact that too few individuals are able to say that they are committed to the experience, to life as experience? It is this retreat from life as experience which causes us to chat rather than speak. The absence of true dialogue, this terrible dryness in communication, this incapacity to communicate makes our conversations only comparable to gossip.

But in order to understand better the dynamic which generates participation and communication, I insist upon the following two points:

a) Experience is preserved by memory. Memory is to guard the experience. I cannot have a dialogue with you unless my experience is well guarded, sheltered like a baby in its mother's womb, and growing within me little by little, as time passes.

b) Experience must be just that, experience. It must be judged by our intelligence. Otherwise, our communication becomes just blabbing out words and vomiting complaints. And how can intelligence judge our experience? It must take the expressive content of our experience and compare it back to the constitutive needs of our humanity, our "elementary experience," which is the essence of intelligence in action.

To summarize: we have pointed out that assuming an unreasonable position before the ultimate questions results in a loss of meaning, which concomitantly, blurs, annuls the personality. This happens because personality emerges as consciousness of a meaning which permits possession and places all aspects of what we meet in relation to their meaning. The annulment of the personality, in its turn, blurs our sense of the past, because we merely "react" to the present. In this way, we burn our bridges with tradition or history, and render sterile our impetus towards the future (though this impetus can remain as anger, an anger directed at nothing, as we read in the *Divine Comedy*: "Flegïas, Flegïas, you cry into a vacuum"[4]). Reactivity reduces our capacity for dialogue and communication, because these are rooted in experience which must be guarded and matured by the memory and judged by intelligence according to those characteristics, those needs which constitute our humanity.

Solitude. Incommunicativeness, the difficulty to communicate, to engage in a dialogue, in turn makes more tragic the solitude that man feels before his own destiny. A terrible sense of solitude overcomes the human being in the face of a destiny devoid of all meaning. Solitude, in fact, does not signify to be alone, but the absence of a meaning. You could stand in the middle of a million people and still be as alone as you can possibly be, if those million people present have no meaning for you.

That solitude which we often lament in our life with others, betrays our misunderstanding of its meaning. We live together failing to recognize what unites us. Thus even the smallest offense becomes a pretense for breaking down the bonds of trust. Conversely, when one is conscious of the adequate reason for being with others, even if everyone else is distracted and uncomprehending, then a person would not be alone at all. For example, when I visit a foreign country, even without knowing the language or a single person, when I enter into a church, my consciousness of a common meaning dissolves my solitude, and renders my action meaningful, profound, solid. Incommunicativeness increases this tragic sense of solitude which the *modern and contemporary* person has in front of a destiny without meaning. Moreover, it also gives it an external shape. In this way, solitude becomes an *exasperating social climate*, sadly the characteristic face of today's society.

So, on the one hand, the heart is gnawed away by a sclerotic hardening, the loss of a person's passion and gusto for living. After all, the substantial attraction for living comes from the past – what a breath of fresh air to read a page of Homer or to repeat verses of Virgil by memory or to remember the plot of a tragedy by Sophocles! The substantial attraction of the present comes from the richness with which it is imbued with its past inheritance. Without this, the present thins out drastically, its attraction becoming as shallow and dry as pure reactivity.

Old age at twenty and even sooner – at fifteen – this is a distinguishing feature of today's world.

The celebrated name of Teilhard de Chardin comes to mind with this tremendous affirmation that the greatest danger which today's humanity need fear is not a catastrophe which comes from out there somewhere, a stellar catastrophe, neither is it famine, nor even disease; rather it is spiritual malady, which is the most terrible malady because the most directly human among the scourges is to remain "without the taste for life."[5] In such a situation, the individual finds himself ever more vulnerable within the social fabric. This is the most dangerous outcome of solitude.

In *Il Compagno*, Cesare Pavese demonstrates such a dramatic vulnerability: "Everyone seeks out the one who can write, everyone wants to talk with him, everyone wants to be able to say tomorrow, 'I know how you are made,' and to make use of him, but no one lends him one day of total sympathy, man to man."[6] Equal to this affirmation is this spine-shivering poem by the clandestine Russian poet, Sergei Chudakov.

> When they cry
>   "Man overboard!"
> the oceanliner, as big as a house,
> stops all at once
> and the man
>   they fish out with the ropes.
> But when
>   a man's soul is overboard,
> when he drowns
> from horror
>   and from desperation
> not even his own household
> stops
> but distances itself.[7]

The individual finds himself ever more vulnerable within the social fabric and at the mercy of the most uncontrolled forces of instinct and power. Solitude becomes so great that the person feels reduced to bits, shredded by a thousand anonymous solicitations. The imagery in this other clandestine Russian poem is persuasive:

> If you have not been in a concentration camp,
> if they have not tortured you,

if your best friend has not written an anonymous letter against you.
If you have not crawled out from a pile of corpses
miraculously escaping the firing squad,
if you do not know the theory of relativity
and of tensor calculus,
if you don't know how to ride a motorcycle at 200 kph,
if you have not killed your loved one following the order of a stranger,
if you don't know how to get semiconductors for a radio,
if you can't, forgetting yourself, cry out hurrah with everyone else,
if you cannot manage to hide yourself within two seconds of an atomic explosion,
if you do not know how to save to clothe yourself by not eating,
if you cannot manage to live in five square meters
and if you don't even play basketball
then you are not a man of the 20th century![8]

This is disintegration!

LOSS OF FREEDOM

The perception of freedom. I stated above that solitude renders the individual at the mercy of the most uncontrolled forces of instinct and power: it is the death of freedom. I would like to linger a while here, even if the discourse, in its entirety, does not appear to justify it.

I would, in fact, like to recall a question of method, because if I were to ask what freedom is, the great majority of people would respond according to images, definitions, or impressions that have been determined by the common mentality. If the definition of life's most important words is determined by this common mentality, then this ensures our total slavery, our complete alienation. What the love between a man and woman is, what fatherhood is, motherhood, what obedience is, companionship, solidarity, friendship, what freedom is – all of these words, in the majority of people, generate an image or opinion or definition taken, literally, from the common mentality, which is the same as saying they are taken from power. This is a slavery from which one does not free oneself automatically. However one can liberate oneself from it with an ascesis, which we have already said is an application of a person's energies in a work upon his "self," intelligence and will.

This is the beginning of freedom. As the ancients said: "intellectus cogitabundus initium omnis bonis"[9] (an intelligence which applies itself is the start of every good). But an intelligence which applies itself intuits, seeks a method, otherwise it could not proceed, because the method is the route. So how do we come to know what freedom is? Words are signs with which a person identifies a specific experience: the word love singles out a certain experience, as does the word freedom. Experience is described, first of all, by an adjective which corresponds to it, because the adjective is a quick and summarizing description of a lived experience; afterwards, the noun ends up being an attempted definition derived from the adjective. Thus, in order to understand what "freedom" is, we must begin with the experience we have of feeling *free*. When does our natural experience, judged according to our elementary needs and "evidences," make us feel free? Perhaps the following will answer this question.

You, daughter, go to your father and say to him, "Will you let me go away for the week-end with my friends?" Your father, his hands full with so much work and many other concerns, has always held the opinion that modern man must be permissive with his children. Therefore, to you, young lady, he has never, not even one single time in living memory, said no. That evening, however, driven crazy by his secretary, he answers, "No, you are not going!" It would be impossible for you not to feel oppressed, imprisoned, suffocated, without freedom. If, on the other hand, you are unsure of your father's answer and he replied, "Yes, by all means go!" your experience of freedom would have been greater because your desire was strong.

Experientially we feel free when we satisfy a desire. Freedom becomes experience in our existence as the realization of a need, or an aspiration, as fulfilment. And it is in this sense of the word that we find the truth in that trite phrase: "being free is doing your own thing." Imagine not just being free for a week-end, an evening, on one hundred, two hundred, a thousand occasions, but always – to be really free, that is to say to experience *freedom*, not just a moment of freedom. Experience indicates that freedom presents itself to us as a total satisfaction, complete fulfilment of the self, as perfection. Or we can say that freedom is the capacity for the end, totality, for *happiness*.

Complete self-fulfilment, this is freedom. Freedom, for the human being, is the possibility, the capacity, the responsibility to be fulfilled, that is to say to reach and confront one's destiny: it is the total aspiration for destiny. Thus freedom is the experience of the truth of ourselves.

It is for this reason that the Lord says, "The truth will set you free" (John 8:32). If God is the truth, then I can say to God: you are my truth, you are my self, I am you; to paraphrase Shakespeare in *Romeo and Juliet* "Thou art me, I am thee."[10] An Other is this truth about myself: this fullness of my being is You, my meaning is You. Therefore, freedom is the capacity for God. Much more deeply than a capacity for choosing, freedom is the humble, passionate, faithful, and total dedication to God in daily life. "God, lover of life," says the liturgy. The faith is the fundamental gesture of freedom, and prayer is the perpetual education of the heart, the spirit in being authentically human, in being free, because faith and prayer are the full recognition of that Presence which is my destiny; and the dependence on this presence is my freedom.

Existentially this freedom is not yet fulfilled. Rather it represents a state of tension towards fulfilment, being, and progressive adhesion. This freedom is in a state of becoming.

Freedom's precarious condition. Let us take note of freedom's original essence. We shall do this by representing all reality which can be experienced with the following figure.

There is nothing within this figure. Now, observe the same figure with a small point inside.

This small point is you. It is I. First you were not there, and now you are.

But what does it mean to speak of freedom, if before this point it did not exist, and if it emerges *totally* as an emerging moment, as a fleeting crest of an enormous wave, of this huge torrent that is the world and history (represented by the circle)? If this point is born totally as a part of that reality in a state of becoming, as a result of its physical and biological antecedents, it has no rights before that reality – the latter can do what it wants with the point, like an impetuous torrent tossing a pebble.

But this world, this reality, on a human level, is called *humanity*. Humanity is still an abstract concept, because humanity, in concrete terms, is called *society*. But society is a certain organic and determined order. And it is through those in *power* that this order is maintained. Even a government, in fact, shapes society because of the power it has.

Now, this little point in the circle (that is, you and I!), has no rights in front of this power. None. This is because power is the prevailing expression of a determined instant of historical flux. Any conception whatsoever of the human person which is pantheistic, materialistic, biological, or idealistic – any of these – must reach these conclusions: in this sense Hitler or Stalin are the same. Power is the emergence of the force of reality in this instant. If, in order to make its contribution to history, power is persuaded that it must kill all Jews, then, according to the conception we mentioned above, it would be justified in killing them or using them all as guinea pigs. The entire reality of our epoch has codified this: the State, whether it be capitalist or Marxist, is the source of every right. But this is not just true of our era. Two thousand years ago, the only man who had all human rights was the *civis romanus*, the Roman citizen. But who decided who was a *civis romanus*? Those in power.

One of the greatest Roman jurists, Gaius, defined three levels of tools which the *civis*, who had full rights, could possess: tools which do not move and do not speak; those which move and do not speak, which is to say, animals; and those which move and speak, the slaves. In this demarcation, freedom as an essential dimension of the person is totally absent.[11]

If one reads the following definition of education given by Anton Makarenko, the most famous Soviet pedagogue, one perceives with horror the hypothetical consequences of state theorization, directed by the heads of the Party, which has the right to possess and to determine the existence of the human being in the same way that a mechanic owns a bolt in his car: "Education is the assembly line from which will exit the product of behavior suited to the requirements of those who systematically embody and interpret the sense of historical process."[12] "Those who systematically embody and interpret the sense of historical process" are the ones who hold power at that moment: this spells the total alienation of the human being within an ideological conception of society brandished by the powers that be.

It is with sadness that the 1980 Nobel Prize winner for poetry, Czeslaw Milosz, made this denunciation:

Man has been given to understand
that he lives only by the grace of those in power.
Let him therefore busy himself sipping coffee, catching butterflies.
Who cares for the Republic will have his right hand cut off.[13]

The foundation of freedom. The Church alone, in its tradition, defends the absolute value of the person, from the first instant of conception to the last moment of old age, however decrepit and useless the individual may be. And what is this defence of the human being's value based on? How is it that man has this right, this absoluteness whereby even if the whole world were to move in one direction he has something within which gives him the right to stay where he is? He has something within by which he or she can judge the world from which he or she was born.

If the human being were to come into the world solely through the biology of the mother and father, as a mere brief instant in which all the flux of innumerable prior reactions produced this ephemeral fruit; if the human being were only this, then we really would be talking about something ridiculous, something cynically absurd when we use expressions such as "freedom," "human rights," the very word, "person." Freedom, like this, without any foundation, is *flatus vocis*, just pure sound, dispersed by the wind.

In only one case is this point in the circle, this single human being, free from the entire world, free, so that the world together and even the total universe cannot force him into anything. In only one instance can this image of a free man be explained. This is when we assume that this point is not totally the fruit of the biology of the mother and father, not strictly derived from the biological tradition of mechanical antecedents, but rather when it possesses a direct relationship with the *infinite*, the *origin* of all of the flux of the world, of the whole "circle" (see previous figure), that is to say, it is endowed with something derived from God.

The Catechism of Pius X affirms this: "the body is given by the parents, but the soul is infused directly by God."[14] Apart from the scholastic formulation, this "soul" indicates precisely that there is a "something" in me which is not derived from any empirical phenomenon, because it does not depend upon, does not originate in the biology of my father and mother. It directly depends on the infinite, which makes the whole world. *Only* this hypothesis allows me to proclaim that the world can do what it wants with me, but it cannot conquer, possess, grasp on to me, because I am greater than it is. I am *free*.

It is here that we find the foundation and the explanation for the fundamental right of freedom of conscience. The human being has not only the capacity, but also the duty to judge and act according to ultimate personal comparison to the truth and the good.

So here is the *paradox*: freedom is dependence upon God. It is a paradox, but it is absolutely clear. The human being – the concrete human person, me, you – once we were not, now we are, and tomorrow will no longer be: thus we depend. And either we depend upon the flux of our material antecedents, and are consequently slaves of the powers that be, or we depend upon What lies at the origin of the movement of all things, *beyond* them, which is to say, God.

Freedom identifies itself with dependence upon God at a human level: it is a recognized and lived dependence, while slavery, on the other hand, denies or censures this relationship. Religiosity is the lived awareness of this relationship. Freedom comes through religiosity. Religiosity is the single hindrance, limit, confine to the dictatorship of man over man, whether we are referring to men and women, parents and children, government and citizens, owners and workers, party chiefs, and rank and file. It is the *only* hindrance, the single barrier and objection to the slavery imposed by the powers that be.

It is for this reason that the powerful, whoever they might be – within the family or a collective – are tempted to hate true religiosity, unless they are profoundly religious themselves. So, for example, nothing in the relationship between a man and a woman is more feared and hated, unconsciously, than an authentic religiosity in the other, because it limits, it challenges possession.

I remember the impression that was made upon me a good number of years ago by an article that appeared on the feature page of a major Italian daily. It was written by the scientist Julian Huxley and was published a short time after the press had launched a great campaign against neonazism after swastikas had appeared on the walls along the streets in Milan. This reminded people of Dachau and Auschwitz, the massacre of man, and the negation of a humane civilization. The piece advocated the possibility and the necessity of controlling births to eliminate all imperfect types and create a perfect human. Who would have established the criteria and the limits for such a project? Ultimately it would be the ruling powers, exactly as in the Nazi system.

The great Boris Pasternak said: "It's a good thing when a man is different from your image of him. It shows he isn't a type. If he were, it would be the end of him as a man."[15] He was referring to an image of the human being as a slave of the powers that be. Without the protection of a relationship with God, the human being is at the mercy of concepts both useful to and fostered by the powerful.

The Italian journalist, Alberto Ronchey, commenting on Solzhenitsyn, correctly recalled the fact that in Shakespeare, Macbeth was a criminal because he killed seven people. "In order to kill six million, or sixty million, one needs a multiplier: this multiplier of crime is ideology,"[16] an all-encompassing conception of the human being fostered by the ruling powers.

If Lenin says – "It is the hour in which it is no longer possible to listen to music, because music arouses the desire to caress children's heads, while the moment has come to cut them off"[7] – then is it with these conceptions that we confront the adventure of defending the human being? But if this human being, this single person is not a direct relationship with the infinite, then whatever those in power do is justified. For this reason, Christ, in the Gospel, exalted his relationship with children, the sick, the old, the public sinners, the poor, the people who were mocked, that is to say, those socially incapable of defending themselves. That Jesus extolled these relationships means this: even those most incapable of defense have an absolute, sacred value. Rather than harm one single hair of their heads, it would be better that one "put a mill-stone around his neck and throw himself to the bottom of the sea" (Matt. 18:6). And where has the absolute dignity of the human person been affirmed with more peremptory drama than in the sentence already cited: "What profit would a man show if he were to gain the whole world and destroy himself in the process? What can a man offer in exchange for his very self?" (Matt. 16:26).

Love counters power, and the divine affirms the human being's capacity for freedom, an irreducible capacity for perfection, for attaining happiness – for meeting the Other, God. The divine is love, as this splendid poem by Tagore witnesses:

By all means they try to hold me secure who love me in this world. But it is otherwise with thy love which is greater than theirs, and thou keepest me free.

Lest I forget them they never venture to leave me alone. But day passes by after day and thou are not seen.

If I call not thee in my prayers, if I keep not thee in my heart, thy love for me still waits for my love.[18]

9 Preconception, Ideology, Rationality, and the Religious Sense

PRECONCEPTIONS: CLARIFICATIONS

If the consequences of negation are so contrary to nature, why do human beings abandon themselves to these positions? It seems to me that there is but one adequate answer: it is because of the domination of *preconception,* the tyranny of prejudice.

It would not be useless to restate a few observations which have already been made. But, first of all, we must make distinctions.

a) There is, as we have seen, a positive meaning of the word "preconception," and this is to be found in its etymological sense. Indeed, when faced with any type of proposal, the human person *reacts,* and he does so on the basis of what he knows and is. In fact, the more pronounced an individual's personality and knowledge, then the more that person will in any encounter whatever immediately sense the formation of a clear image, idea, judgment. Inevitably a preconception arises in front of anything and everything.

b) The negative sense of the term "preconception" manifests itself when the human being's *criterion* for judging a proposed reality is his inevitable reaction. In this case, the preconception is not just conditioning to be overcome in an *openness of asking* (refer this statement to our discussion of the morality of knowing in chapter three). In fact, overcoming a preconception allows you to reach a meaning that transcends your present knowledge (or what you think you know). "Men do not learn when they believe they already know," says Barbara Ward.[1]

One time, while teaching, in order to stir up my students, I wrote on the board, "RAU" ("UAR" in English). One boy exclaimed, "You are always being political!" It was, indeed, during the time in which the Reppublica Araba Unita (the United Arab Republic) was formed. Another student asked, "What does it mean?" And I answered, "This is not read as 'RAU,' but as 'chai,' and it means 'tea' in Russian." The first comment, made by one of the most "politicized" students in the class, had judged me according to his political preconception in which he was hermetically sealed; the second was instinctively open, and, by asking a question, the student had placed himself in the potential position of being able to learn something new.

For our purposes, an obstructive preconception has two principal roots:

1) Materialistic prejudice. This is the position described in this quotation by the extremely youthful (seventeen-year-old!) Cesare Pavese: "Once having taken up materialism, there is no longer any going forward ... I struggle to pull myself up; but I convince myself only the more that there is nothing to be done."[2]

2) "Preconception's social self-defense."

This stance seems to me to be pointed out very well in this passage from Plato's *Gorgias:*

Callicles: I can't explain it, Socrates, but I do think you're making your points well. All the same, I'm feeling what people invariably feel with you: I'm not entirely convinced.

Socrates: It's the demotic love [attachment to the common mentality of the populace] residing in your heart which is resisting me, Callicles.[3]

IDEOLOGY

Ideology is a theoretical–practical construction developed from a preconception. More precisely, it is a theoretical–practical construction based upon an *aspect* of reality – even a true aspect – which is formulated for the aims of a philosophy or political project, is taken unilaterally and made, in principle, into an absolute. And, since ideology is built upon some starting point of our experience, experience itself is used as a pretext for an operation determined by extraneous concerns. For example,in front of the "poor" one can theorize about the problem of poverty. But the concrete person with his or her real wants becomes marginalized once he has been used as a pretext, the starting point for the intellectual and his or her opinions, or by the politician to justify and publicize his own platform. The views of intellectuals, which the powers that be find convenient and take up as their own, become the common mentality by means of the mass-media, schools, and propaganda. Rosa Luxemburg, with revolutionary lucidity, stigmatized such a process as "the creeping advance of the theoretician" which gnaws at the root of and corrupts every authentic impetus and change.

A classic example of this social dynamic is amply documented in the materialistic prejudice against religion. I want to cite a quotation from the noted scientist, Pierre Lecomte du Noüy, taken from his famous book *L'Avenir de l'esprit*.

Those who, without any proof (as has been demonstrated elsewhere) are systematically forced to destroy the idea of God, have done cowardly and unscientific work.

I proclaim this with all the more force and conviction in as much as I do not possess the Faith, that truth, which gushes forth from deep within our being. I do not believe in God more than I believe in the reality of evolution or the reality of electrons. ... And I have the scientific certainty of not being mistaken. Far from being (as other men of science whom I envy) supported and aided by an unshakable faith in God, I went into life with a destructive scepticism that was very much in fashion in those days. I had to spend thirty years in the laboratory in order to arrive at the point of being convinced that those who had had the duty of enlightening me, if only by confessing to me their ignorance, had instead deliberately lied to me. My conviction today is rational. I have arrived at it by the pathways of biology and physics and am persuaded that it is impossible for any man of science who reflects not to arrive at this point, unless it be because of blindness or bad faith. But the path that I followed is a tortuous one and not a good one. And it is so that others may avoid the immense loss of time and the fatigue that I have suffered that I now rise up against the evil spirit of the bad shepherds.[4]

Solzhenitsyn, in his great novel, *Cancer Ward,* taking his cue from the philosopher Bacon, analytically details the various mechanisms of man's alienating dependence upon the *de facto* dominant ideology.

Francis Bacon set out his doctrine of idols back in the sixteenth century. He said people are not inclined to live by pure experience, that it's easier for them to pollute experience with prejudices. These prejudices are the idols. "The idols of the tribe," Bacon called them. "the idols of the cave."

The idols of the theatre are the authoritative opinions of others which a man likes to accept as a guide when interpreting something he hasn't experienced himself ... Another idol of the theatre is our overwillingness to agree with the arguments of science. One can sum this up as the voluntary acceptance of other people's errors! The idols of the market place are the errors which result from the communication and association of men with each other. They are the errors a man commits because it has become customary to use certain phrases and formulas which do violence to reason.

For example, "Enemy of the people!" "Not one of us!" "Traitor!" Call a man one of these and everyone will renounce him.[5]

REASON

Preconception confines itself to the familiar and expected, while ideology tends to attribute an aura of redemption and salvation to outlooks and practices which are well determined, dominated, and manipulated: "scientific," they say. Yet the most gravely serious research today testifies clearly against the reductive process of pre-conception and ideology.

The scientific attitude – in the proper sense of the term – we already know cannot be the exhaustive approach to experience. Indeed, it is precisely "through experience" that we know that there are dimensions and phenomena which do not reduce themselves to either the physical–chemical or biological spheres. Experience itself, in its totality, leads to the authentic comprehension of the term *reason* or rationality. Indeed, reason is that singular event of nature in which it – reason – reveals itself as the operative need to explain reality *in all of its factors* so that the human being is introduced to the truth about things. In this way, reality emerges within experience and rationality illuminates the factors within it. To say "rational" is to affirm the transparency or intelligibility of human experience, its substance and depth. Rationality is critical transparency, of our human experience: "critical" means according to an all-encompassing view.

Let us insist: the essential characteristic of the human being is a self-transparency – self-awareness – and an awareness of the whole horizon of reality.

As we have already seen, "rational" is not what can be measured or fit into a dialectic. A great contemporary French philosopher, Paul Ricoeur, in this perfect sentence, has pointed out the essence of reason – its unexhausted openness before the unexhausted call of the real: "That which I am is incommensurable with what I know."

To re-emphasize this point: if we posit a concept which is not demonstrated by our integral experience, then we can pursue logical discourses, volume after volume. However, this is outside of reality. The following letter sent to me by a student demonstrates this:

What can I say to a person like my father who holds that questions about life's meaning are senseless? According to my father, a person can, at best, ask himself: "What goal do I want to give to my life? To whom and to what do I want to devote my energy?" Questions like, "Ultimately what sense does my life make? Why do I live, why am I here, and where will I end up?", are nonsense, because a person is a fool if he thinks that he has a meaning. And, according to my father, if one wants to give some meaning to the world starting from himself, the example would be the following: "Wouldn't it seem strange to you if a rock were to ask you why it exists? It's there, and that's that, its presence has no meaning." Thus the person within the universe is a very miserable and miniscule particle which has no meaning. According to my father, one needs to free oneself from the desire to be at the centre of the world and to accept our situation, to accept what we are. Because I am not happy with this, he says that I am a dreamer and that I don't make sense, that it does not build my personality to drag myself for years through these questions which I don't know how to answer. I understand how inhuman this position is, but I don't know how to answer him. My father's arguments appear to me to be logical and rational.

I would like to ask that man: "Why would those questions, if they reflect an openness inherent to our nature, be nonsense?" There is, it seems to me, only one answer: because he says so! He casts his shadow upon the light of the heart. This, exactly this, is preconception. And, of course, a rock does not ask itself: "Why do I exist?" It does not, precisely because it is a rock and not a human being. The human being, on the other hand, is properly that level of nature in which nature asks itself: "Why do I exist?" Man is that miniscule particle which demands a meaning, a reason – the reason. And if we accept what we are, we cannot censure this desire which urges us on like a spur. This question exists within the self, and since the answer is greater than a person's capacity to grasp and imagine it, then, to define such an answer as "illusion" is to repeat Aesop's fable of the fox and the grapes.

The arguments of that man might very well be logical, but they are not rational, precisely because they are based on a preconception. They do not develop according to the indications of experience, and they do not follow experience's ultimate and decisive invitation. At the culmination of his questioning, he denies and censures.

THE RELIGIOUS SENSE AND RATIONALITY

The religious sense lives by this rationality and is its face, its most authentic expression. Andrey Sinyavsky affirms this in his *Unguarded Thoughts:* "One must have faith not because of tradition, or out of fear of death, or 'just in case,' or because one has been ordered to or something frightens one, or out of humanistic principles, or in order to be saved, or for the sake of originality. One must have faith for the simple reason that God *is.*"[6]

The religious sense appears as a first and most authentic application of the term *reason* because it never ceases responding relentlessly to reason's most basic need, for meaning. In his *Tractatus,* Wittgenstein affirms that "the meaning of life, that is to say the meaning of the world, we can call God. To pray is to think about the meaning of life."[7]

Only in a religious dimension is it possible to intuit reason or the whole structural dynamic of consciousness (or reason): 1) because reason asks about meaning, which is like saying the ultimate sum or the ultimate intensity of all of the factors of reality; and 2) because it opens us to and sets us on the threshold of what is *different, other,* infinite.

Kant intuits this in an unforgettable page of *Critique of Pure Reason;*

Human reason has this peculiar fate that in one species of its knowledge it is burdened by questions which, as prescribed by the very nature of reason itself, it is not able to ignore, but which, as transcending all its powers, it is not able to answer. The perplexity into which it thus falls is not due to any fault of its own. It begins with principles which it has no option save to employ in the course of experience ... Rising with their aid (since it is determined to do this by its own nature) to ever higher, ever more remote, conditions, it soon becomes aware that in this way – the questions never ceasing – its work must always remain incomplete; and it therefore finds itself compelled to resort to principles which overstep all possible empirical employment ... they are no longer subject to any empirical test.[8]

But the fact that reason feels itself "compelled" to seek out other principles is a "constraint" implied in experience, a factor of experience itself. To deny this step is to go against experience. It is to disown something implied in it.

If one does not accept such an implication then one can only fall back into ideology and preconception.

10 How the Ultimate Questions Arise: The Way of the Religious Sense

A new perspective on the problem awaits us.

If those ultimate questions are the very essence, the stuff of human consciousness, human reason, how do they arise? To answer such a question, we must identify how a person reacts to reality. If an individual becomes aware of his constitutive factors by observing himself in action, we need to observe this human dynamic in its impact with reality, an impact which sets in motion the mechanism revealing these factors. If an individual were to barely live the impact with reality, because, for example, he had not had to struggle, he would scarcely possess a sense of his own consciousness, would be less aware of his reason's energy and vibration.

In the following description the factors of this mechanism, in a certain sense, assemble themselves in a chronological sequence.

AWE OF THE "PRESENCE"

First of all, to make myself understood, I will stir your imagination. Picture yourself being born, coming out of your mother's womb at the age you are now at this very moment in terms of your development and consciousness. What would be the first, absolutely your initial reaction? If I were to open my eyes for the first time in this instant, emerging from my mother's womb, I would be overpowered by the wonder and awe of things as a "presence." I would be bowled over and amazed by the stupefying repercussion of a presence which is expressed in current language by the word "thing." Things! That's "something!" "Thing," which is a concrete and, if you please, banal version of the word "being." *Being:* not as some abstract entity, but as presence, a presence which I do not myself make, which I find. A presence which imposes itself upon me.

He who does not believe in God is inexcusable, says St Paul in his letter to the Romans (Rom. 1:19–21), because that person must deny this original phenomenon, this original experience of the "other." A baby lives this experience without being aware of it, because he is not yet completely conscious. But the adult who does not live it or does not consciously perceive it, is less than a baby. That person is atrophied.

The awe, the marvel of this reality which imposes itself upon me, of this presence which reaches me is at the origin of the awakening of human consciousness. "Radical amazement is to the understanding of the realness of God what clarity and distinctness are to the comprehension of mathematical ideas ... Devoid of wonder, we remain deaf to the sublime."[1]

Therefore, the very first sense of the human being is that of facing a reality which is not his, which exists independently of him, and upon which he depends. Empirically translated, it is the original perception of a *given,* a word which, if used in a completely human sense, involving the total person, all of the factors of an individual's personality, comes alive: "given," as a past participle, implies something which "gives." The word which translates in the content of human terms the word "given," and thus describes the content of our first impact with reality, is the word *gift*. But without dwelling on this, the very word "given" is also vibrant with an activity, in front of which I am passive: and it is a passivity which makes up my original activity of receiving, taking note, recognizing.

One time, while I was teaching in a high school, I asked: "So then, according to you, what does "evidence" mean? Can one of you define it?" One boy, to the right of my chair, after a very long and embarrassed silence on the part of the students, exclaimed: "But then evidence is an inexorable presence!" Becoming aware of an inexorable presence! I open my eyes to this reality which imposes itself upon me, which does not depend upon me, but upon which I depend; it is the great conditioning of my existence – if you like, the given. It is this awe which awakens the ultimate question within us: not as a cold observation, but as a wonder pregnant with an attraction, almost a passivity in which simultaneously is conceived an attraction.

There is no attitude more retrograde than a certain claimed scientific approach towards religion and humanity, in general. It is, indeed, truly superficial to repeat that religion is born of fear. Fear is not a human being's first sentiment – it is attraction. Fear emerges only in a second moment, as a reflex to a perceived danger that this attraction may be fleeting. Attachment to being, to life, awe in front of the evidence comes first: only after this is it possible for one to fear that this evidence might vanish, that the presence might not be yours, that the attraction you feel might not be fulfilled. You do not fear losing things which do not interest you. Rather, you fear losing things which have to interest you first.

Religiosity is, first of all, the affirmation and development of the attraction. A true seeker's disposition is laden with a prior evidence and an awe: the wonder of the presence attracts me, and that is how the search within me breaks out. Fear is a shadow which descends upon us as a second reaction. You fear losing something, even when you have had it only for an instant.

Another great word which must intervene to clarify further the meaning of "given," is "other, otherness." Let us take up again our image: if I were to be born with the consciousness that I now have, and my eyes were, for the first time, to fly open, then reality would disclose itself as the presence of something "other" than myself. "Religious awe is something other than the wonder from which, according to Aristotle, philosophy is born. When otherness emerges before one's eyes, the human person is not given to posing speculative inquiries, but to venerating, to pleading, to entreating, to invoking, to contemplating. This remains firm, that it is the different-from-oneself and the meta- (=beyond) natural."[2]

The human being's original dependence is well explained in the Bible, in chapters thirty-eight and thirty-nine of the Book of Job, in the dramatic dialogue ("duel") between God and Job. After the latter has given into a rebellious lament, for two chapters, God presses on with his radical questions, as Job appears physically to shrink, as if he wants to vanish because he is absolutely unable to give an answer. Then, from the heart of the tempest, Yahweh gives Job his answer:

> Who is obscuring my designs
>   with his empty-headed words?
> Brace yourself like a fighter;
>   now it is my turn to ask questions and your turn
>   to inform me.
> Where were you when I laid the earth's foundations?
>   Tell me, since you are so well informed!
> Who decided the dimensions of it, do you know?
>   Or who stretched the measuring line across it?

What supports its pillars at their bases?
  Who laid its cornerstone
when all the stars of the morning were singing with
    joy?[3]

Nothing is more adequate to the nature of the human person than his original dependence. Indeed, the human being is, by nature created.

We can say then, that three different nuances make up this first factor: The first is reality perceived as "otherness" or the "given," as "thing," generally speaking. In the second, only in a subsequent moment do I distinguish faces and things in this reality. And, in the third, I become aware of myself, therefore only later making distinctions and finally perceiving this "I" as distinct from other things. The psychological trajectory of the human being confirms this because the perception of the "I" as "distinct from" comes at a certain point in the evolution of one's consciousness. One comes to understand oneself as a "given," as "made," and this is the last step within the perception of reality as "thing" and "things."

The prime original intuition then, is the awe in front of this given and of the "I" as part of it. First you are struck, and then comes the recognition that you have been struck. It is from this that the idea of life as gift originates: without this concept, everything man touches turns to dust.

THE COSMOS

The human person, having become aware of this real "being," this inexorable presence with its diversities, and of his own "I" as a part of it, also realizes that within this reality there is an *order*, that this reality is cosmic (from the Greek word "cosmos," which means, in fact, order).

Kant once confessed that the moment in which he doubted his *Critique of Practical Reason* – the book which denied that one can move from reality on to another presence – was when he went out from his house and, lifting up his head, gazed at the starry sky.[4]

For all men were by nature foolish who were in ignorance of God,
  and who from the good things seen did not succeed in knowing him
who is,
  and from studying the works did not discern the artisan:
But either fire, or wind, or the swift air, or the
  circuit of the stars, or the mighty water,

or the luminaries of heaven, the governors
of the world, they considered gods.
Now if out of joy in their beauty they thought them gods,
let them know how far more excellent is the Lord than these;
for the original source of beauty fashioned them.
For from the greatness and the beauty of created things
their original author, by analogy, is seen.[5]

Thus, the original awe implies a sense of beauty, the attraction of harmonious beauty. We will better define, afterwards, the value of the word "analogy," as cited in the biblical passage.

"PROVIDENTIAL" REALITY

Not only does the human being recognize this inexorable presence as beautiful and attractive, harmoniously ordered, corresponding with him, he also sees that this reality moves itself according to a plan which can be favourable to him. It makes day and night, morning and evening, autumn, winter, summer, and spring; it establishes the cycles by which the human being can rejuvenate, refresh, sustain, and reproduce himself.

The more ancient religions reflect the experiences of reality as "providential." The relationship with the divine (around which doctrines and rites developed) was based upon the mystery of fertility – of the earth and woman. This sense of providential reality is fore- shadowed, first of all by God in the following passage from the Bible, after the flood:

When the Lord smelled the sweet odor, he said to himself: Never again will I doom the earth because of man, since the desires of man's heart are evil from the start; nor will I ever again strike down all living beings, as I have done.

As long as the earth lasts
cold and heat, seedtime and harvest,
summer and winter
and day and night
shall not cease.[6]

And it is this that St Paul is alluding to in his speech in Listra in Asia Minor, when, after having performed a miracle, all of the people, including the priests of the temple of Zeus, go there, to him and Barnabas, greeting them with incense and incense burners, because they believed Paul to be Hermes (the smaller God) and Barnabas (taller and stronger) to be Zeus, who had arrived in the city.

Friends, why do you do this? ... We are only men, human like you, We are bringing you the good news that will convert you from just such follies as these to the living God, 'the one who made heaven and earth and the sea and all that is in them.' In past ages he let the Gentiles go their way. Yet in bestowing his benefits, he has not hidden himself completely, without a clue. From the heavens he sends down rain and rich harvests; your spirits he fills with food and delight.[7]

These are the marks of every ancient religion's original discourse: the sense of the divine as *providence*.

THE DEPENDENT "I"

At this point, when an individual is reawakened within his being by the presence, the attraction, the awe, he is grateful, joyful, because this presence can be beneficial and providential. The human being becomes aware of himself as *I*, recovers this original awe with a depth that establishes the measure, the stature of his identity. At this moment, if I am attentive, that is, if I am mature, then I cannot deny that the greatest and most profound evidence is that *I do not make myself*, I am not making myself. I do not give myself being, or the reality which I am. I am "given." This is the moment of maturity when I discover myself to be dependent upon something else.

If I descend to my very depths, where do I spring from? Not from myself: from *something else*. This is the perception of myself as a gushing stream born from a spring, from something else, more than me, and by which I am made. If a stream rushing forth from a spring could think, it would perceive, at the bottom of its fresh surging, an origin it does not know, which is other than itself.

Here we are speaking of the intuition, which, in every period of history, the more intelligent human spirits have had. It is an intuition of this mysterious presence, which endows the instant, the "I" with substance (solidity, density, foundation). *I am you-who-make-me* – except that this *you* is absolutely faceless. I use this word *you* because it is the least inadequate in my experience as a human being to indicate that unknown presence which is beyond comparison, more than my experience as a human being. What other word could I, on the other hand, use? When I examine myself and notice that I am not making myself by myself, then I – with the full and conscious vibration of affection which this word I exudes – turn to the Thing that makes me, to the source that causes me to be in this instant, and I can only address it using the word *you*. *You-who-make-me* is, therefore, what religious tradition calls God – it is that which is more than I, more "I" than I myself. It is that by means of which I am.

For this reason, the Bible says of God: "tam pater nemo," (Gal. 4:6) or, no one is as much a father, because, in our experience, a father gives life its beginning which, from the first fraction of the first instant of being, detaches itself and goes off on its own. A woman expressed this to me in a most surprising way. When I was still a very young priest, this woman would come regularly for confession. For some time I did not see her anymore, and, when she returned, she said to me: "I had a second baby girl." Before I could reply, she added: "I was truly surprised! Just as I became aware that she had been born, I did not think of whether it was a boy or a girl, whether it was healthy or not. No, the first idea that came to mind was this: 'Look here, it is starting to go on its own.'"

Hostia Whereas God, Father in every instant, is conceiving me *now*. No one is so much a father: he who generates.

To be conscious of oneself right to the core is to perceive, at the depths of the self, an Other. This is prayer: to be conscious of oneself to the very centre, to the point of meeting an Other. Thus prayer is the only human gesture which totally realizes the human being's stature.

The "I," the human being, is that level of nature in which nature becomes aware of not being made by itself. In this way, the entire cosmos is like the continuation of my body. But one could also say that the human being is that level of nature in which nature experiences its own *contingency*. Man experiences himself as contingent, subsists by means of something else, because he does not make *opposizione:* himself by himself. I stand on my feet because I lean on another. I am because I am made. Like my voice, which is the echo of a vibration, if I cease the vibration, it no longer exists. Like spring water rising up – it is, in its entirety, derived from its source. And like a flower which depends completely upon the support of its roots. So I do not consciously say "I am," in a sense that captures my entire stature as a human being if I do not mean "I am made." The ultimate equilibrium of life depends upon this. The human being's natural truth, as we have seen, is his nature as creation – he exists because he is continually possessed. And, when he recognizes this, then he breathes fully, feels at peace, glad.

True self-consciousness is well portrayed by the baby in the arms of his mother and father – supported like this, he can enter any situation whatsoever, profoundly tranquil, with a promise of peace and *qualsiasi*

joy. No curative system can claim this, without mutilating the person.
Often, in order to excise the censure of certain wounds we end up
censuring our humanity. *fenta   sl finisce per*

All human actions, therefore, inasmuch as they aim toward peace
and joy, seek God, the exhaustive substance of our lives.

THE LAW OF THE HEART

But, at this point, there is a final vivid meaning at the very interior of
this *I*, this *I* realized as "made by," "relying on," "contingent upon," a
quivering within, a voice which says "good" and "bad," this consciousness of the "I" which carries with it the perception of good and evil.
Both the Old Testament and St Paul define this as "the law written
within our hearts" (Rom. 2:15). The source of our being places
within us the vibration of good and the suggestion, the remorse of
evil. There is a voice within us. It calls to mind this poem by Giovanni
Pascoli:

> There is a voice in my life,
> I hear it as it dies away;
> a tired, lost voice,
> with the quivering of a beating heart.
>
> A pining voice.
> It grasps at poor lips
> to say many, then many things,
> but its mouth is full of dirt.[8]

This poem refers to the voice of the poet's mother, and describes
how we treat the Voice of our "I": we suffocate it with the dirt of our
distractions and our worries.

The experience of the "I" carries with it the consciousness of good
and evil, an awareness that certain things must be either approved or
rejected. No matter what, this ability to judge, to distinguish between
good and evil cannot be eradicated because it responds to an ultimate destination, our nexus with destiny. It is something which
imposes itself upon me, obliges me to judge and recognize something
as either good or evil. It is the path used by the Creator to draw to
itself all of our existence. It is a path of something good, of something right to which is attached the meaning of life itself, of one's
own existence, of the real; which is good and *right* because it is so, not
at the mercy of anything, of infinite value. That a mother loves her
child, this is good because it is good; that someone's self-sacrifice

helps a stranger is good, because it is good. St Paul said in his letter to the Romans: "When the Gentiles who do not have the law keep it as by instinct, these men although without the law serve as a law for themselves. They show that the demands of the law are written in their hearts. Their conscience bears witness together with that law, and their thoughts will accuse or defend them ..." (Rom. 2:14–15).

Even a pagan, the great poet Sophocles, in *Antigone,* spoke of the sacred limits of the law:

All your strength is weakness itself against
The immortal unrecorded laws of God.
They are not merely now: they were, and shall be,
Operative for ever, beyond man utterly.[9]

CONCLUSION

What is the formula for the journey to the ultimate meaning of reality? Living the real. There is an experience, hidden yet implied, of that arcane, mysterious presence to be found within the opening of the eye, within the attraction reawakened by things, within the beauty of things, within an amazement, full of gratitude, comfort, and hope. And this is so because these things move themselves in such a way that they serve me, are useful to me. Numbered among these things is myself as well – myself, in whom that presence which is concealed, hidden, becomes close, because it is here, forming me but also informing me of good and evil.

Now the question is this: How can this complex, yet simple, this enormously rich experience of the human heart – which is the heart of the human person and, therefore, of nature, the cosmos – how can it become vivid, how can it come alive? How can it become powerful? In the *"impact" with the real.* The only condition for being truly and faithfully religious, the formula for the journey to the meaning of reality is to live always the real intensely, without preclusion, without negating or forgetting anything. Indeed, it would not be human, that is to say, reasonable, to take our experience at face value, to limit it to just the crest of the wave, without going down to the core of its motion.

The positivism that dominates modern man excludes the call emanating from our original relationship with things, to search for meaning. This relationship invites us to seek substance, a meaning and enables us to sense this presence that provides substance which things themselves are not. This is so true that I (and it is here that the problem is defined), I myself am not this presence either, because I am the level where the stars and the earth become aware of their own lack of substance. Positivism excludes the invitation to discover the meaning addressed to us precisely by our original and immediate impact with reality. It would have us accept appearances. And this is suffocating.

The more one lives this level of consciousness in his relationship with things, the more intense the impact with reality, and the more one begins to know mystery.

Let us repeat: a trivial relationship with reality, whose most symptomatic aspect is preconception, blocks the authentic religious dimension, the true religious fact. The mark of great souls and persons who are truly alive is an eagerness for this search, carried out through their commitment to the reality of their existence.

Here then is the conclusion: we could say that the world, this reality into which we collide unleashes a word, an invitation, a meaning as if upon impact. The world is like a word, a "logos" which sends you further, calls you on to another, beyond itself, further up. In Greek "up" is expressed with the word *ana*. This is the value of *analogy:* the structure of the "impact" of the human being with reality awakens within the individual a voice which draws him towards a meaning which is further on, further up – *ana*.

Analogy: this word sums up the dynamic structure of the human being's "impact" with reality.

11 The Experience of the Sign

important

Living the real is
a really revolution

MEttors :   the (an food this
Destiny   for the absurd

more
like a

The way reality strikes me demonstrates the existence of some other thing. But how? How does the phenomenon we described in the last chapter demonstrate this?

PROVOCATION

First of all, it is clear that the awe which we have described constitutes an *experience of provocation*. Upon gazing at reality, I have before me something which produces openness. Reality presents itself to me in a way that solicits me to pursue something else. I do not react to reality as a photographic film upon which reality "impresses" its image and that's that. Not only does reality make an impression upon me, it also moves me and solicits me to engage in a search for some other thing, something beyond immediate appearances. It latches on to my consciousness, enabling it to pre-sense and perceive something else. Faced with the sea, the earth, the sky, and all things moving within them, I am not impassive – I am animated, moved, and touched by what I see. And this motion is towards a search for something else.

I can express this reaction with questions: What is this in front of me? Why this? A kind of strange unknown lies within such questions: the world, the real provokes me towards an other. Otherwise one would not ask why, how. I do not simply record everything my consciousness encounters. Rather, I am entirely perturbed by this relationship with the real, pushed beyond the immediate.

A poetic interpretation of this tension which reality arouses in the

human person appears in the vibrant analogy of expectation, the
theme of a beautiful poem by Clemente Rebora:

> From the taut image
> I keep watch upon the instant
> with imminence of expectancy
> and I expect no one:
> in the lighted shadow
> I spy the bell
> that scatters an imperceptible
> pollen of sound –
> and I expect no one:
> within four walls
> more entranced by space
> than a desert
> I expect no one:
> but come he must,
> come he will, if I hold out
> blossoming unseen,
> he will come suddenly,
> when I am least aware:
>
> he will come almost as forgiveness
> of so much death that he causes,
> he will come to make me certain
> of his treasure and mine,
> he will come as balm
> of his sorrows and mine,
> he will come, perhaps already is coming:
> his whisper.[1]

THE SIGN

What do we call something which is seen and touched, which moves
me towards something else when I see and touch it? It is called a sign.
The sign, then, is a reality which refers me to something else. The
sign is a reality whose meaning is another reality, something I am able
to experience, which acquires its meaning by leading to another
reality. The sign is nature's method of drawing us on to something
other than itself: the method of the sign.

The sign is also the normal method human beings use in their
relationships – for example, they express their truth and love through
signs. If a Martian, visiting the earth, were to see a mother give a kiss

to her child, he would ask: "What is this gesture?" The reality of this act invites him to discover what it might mean, provokes him toward something else. It is the phenomenon of the sign.

IRRATIONAL DENIAL

It would not be rational, that is to say, in keeping with a human being's nature, to deny the existence of something else, any more than it would be reasonable to limit the meaning of a sign at a cross-roads to a mere pole with an arrow on it. This definition of that object is inadequate, unreasonable that is, not in keeping with the human energy meeting that pole and that arrow – penetrating no further than its immediate appearance and, humanly speaking, an inadequate way to understand it.

Perhaps another illustration will develop my point. Let us say that upon entering your room, I noticed a vase with a bunch of violets in it, and said: "Nice, who gave them to you?" And, when you did not reply, I insisted: "Who put that bouquet there for you?" until finally you answered: "It's there because it's there." As long as you did not directly answer my question, I would be unsatisfied. If, at last, you said, "My mother gave it to me," I would then say, "Ah," appeased. Indeed, to refuse the invitation contained in the vase of flowers to ask where they came from would not be a human way of looking at them. The presence of the vase of flowers is, indeed, a sign of something else.

I will propose another analogy to you. Let us suppose that you and I are walking in the mountains, a bit out of breath because of the hot sun. At a certain point, we hear a cry: "Help!" Our first reaction is to stop. After a second or two, we hear another cry: "Help!" and I take off in the direction of the voice. You, however, stand there indifferently and ask: "What are you doing?" "But someone has cried 'Help!' " I reply. "But no, you heard a vibration in the air, which echoed h-e-l-p; you heard these four sounds. You cannot deduce from this that someone is crying out 'Help!'" This would not be a human way to perceive that phenomenon. To confine our understanding of this cry to its immediate perceptible appearance would not be rational.

By analogy, it would not be human to deal with the reality of the world by stifling the human capacity to delve ever more deeply into this search for something else, because, as human beings, we are invited by the presence of things to engage in this search. This would be, as we have already said, the positivist position: the total blocking out of the human.

Those ultimate needs of which we have spoken are nothing other than the acting out of that inexhaustible attempt to search for an answer to the questions why? and how? This never comes to an end.

LIFE AS NEED

I want to develop this last point. There is experiential evidence that the nature of the human being's "impact" with the real develops this sense of presentiment, or search, for an other. This evidence is given by the fact that life's structure, the structure of the existential experience is *need*. Life is made up of a fabric of interwoven needs, which can be broken down into two fundamental categories: the need for truth and justice. Both of these categories have important corollaries that could be listed as original classes by themselves, and they are the need for happiness and love.

a) The first category, the need for *truth*, is, simply to say, the need to understand the meaning of things, of existence. Let us imagine that you had before your eyes a mechanism which you had never seen before, and you were to analyze it as much as you wanted, down to the finest detail of its smallest components. In the end, you could not say that you knew this machine if, after all of this disheartening work, you still did not understand its purpose. Why? Because the machine's truth is its meaning, or, you could say, the answer to this question: "What is its function?" This question seeks the link between all of those bits and pieces that comprise the mechanism and the mechanism taken in its entirety; it attempts to understand its purpose, the rule of the machine in the whole of reality. In this sense then, the more a person inquires into the composition of something, the more exasperated his demand regarding its possible meaning.

The need for truth always implies, then, singling out the ultimate truth, because one can only define a partial truth in relation to the ultimate. Nothing can be known without a quick, implicit comparison, if you like, between the thing and totality. Without even a glimpse of the ultimate perspective, things become monstrous.

The need for truth also implicates, sustains, and shapes even the relentless curiosity with which a person penetrates, evermore deeply, into the structure of the real. Nothing placates this, nothing. "Quid fortius desiderat anima quam veritatem?" said St Augustine ("What does the soul desire with more strength than what is true?").[2] The truth, the real meaning of everything lies in its perceived link with the totality, the depths, the ultimate. This is the supreme longing of that level of nature in which nature becomes "I." One time, Socrates, while giving lessons in the Agora of Athens, at the climax of his dialectic, with all the faces of his disciples dramatically intent upon him, suddenly stopped his train of thought and, suspending his discourse, said: "Friends, is it not perhaps true that when we speak of the truth, we even forget about women?" A society is human, is civilized to the extent that its education helps to maintain fully this insatiable openness, despite all of the conveniences and interests which would want to stifle it prematurely.[3]

Can we imagine that in one hundred, a thousand years, in a billion centuries people will be able to say: "We know everything?" We would be finished as human beings. We would have nothing left to do except kill ourselves. In fact, it is simply impossible to conceive of this. The more a person penetrates into the real, which has irremediably solicited and provoked him, the more he becomes aware of the fact that everything he discovers is, as we have already quoted from Francesco Severi, "in function of an absolute which sets itself in opposition, like an elastic barrier, to its being overcome by cognitive means."[4]

b) The second category, which by nature belongs to the first, is the need for *justice*.

Many years ago, there was a serious debate in the English press about a man who was condemned to death, executed, and subsequently found to be innocent. That poor man had continued to cry out in prison that he was not guilty! Reading about this tragedy, I began to identify with this individual who had gone to the gallows an innocent man. Who would give him justice now? Perhaps we could, by recognizing him as not guilty? But this is no answer for him. It is, rather, for ourselves, to pacify us. We render justice to his memory, or, you could say, to our historic curiosity, but not to him. Who then will give him justice? If he does not receive justice, then justice is not done. The answer is fulfilment of the need for justice that is he. Need is an entreaty which identifies itself with the human being, the person. Without a perspective of a beyond, justice is impossible.

c) The third category is *happiness*, or, the fulfilment of the self. With analogous words, we can speak of total satisfaction (*satis factus*), which is the psychological aspect of fulfilment, or perfection ("made whole"), the ontological echo of self-realization.

Who can fulfil this need for happiness?

I remember a book on Franciscanism by Father Agostino Gemelli (the founder of the Catholic University in Italy). In this book, all of the chapters had the first letter illustrated. For example, one chapter began with the word "quando" (when). The tail of the Q was a little bird and, within the oval of the Q, was a profile of a mountain with a rising sun and the silhouette of Saint Francis of Assisi with his head thrown back and his arms opened wide. This was a symbol of man's sensibility, his impact with the most fascinating aspect of nature. And, at the feet of St Francis, the same Q initiated another sentence: "Quid animo satis?" What satisfies the soul?

It would not be a rational or human way of looking at the experience of this need if one did not perceive within it a reference to Other.

d) The fourth category is *love*.

A passage from *Romeo and Juliet* synthetically expresses the analogical openness of love's dynamism in the human person.

> Show me a mistress that is passing fair,
> what doth her beauty serve but as a note
> where I may read who pass'd that passing
> fair?[5]

The attraction of beauty follows a paradoxical trajectory: the more something is beautiful, the more it refers one on to something else. The greater the art (let us think of music), the more it flings wide open, does not confine desire. It is a sign of something else. "He loves who says to the other: you cannot die." This loving intuition of Gabriel Marcel also refers us on to something else.

Human existence, as need, points to *something beyond itself* as its meaning, its goal. Human needs constitute a reference, an implicit affirmation of an ultimate answer which lies *beyond* the experiential aspects of existence. If the hypothesis of a "beyond" were to be eliminated, those needs would be unnaturally suffocated.

YOU, THE SUPREME SIGN

Any outlook which would stifle the dynamic of the sign and arrest the reference to something else which constitutes the heart of the human experience, would murder what is human, unduly frustrate the impetus of a living dynamism.

Imagine the grotesque scene of a baby who, following a shipwreck, finds himself deposited upon the usual deserted island that we read about in the comics, with banana trees and the like. And suppose that this baby, fed by those fruits sprouting up everywhere or by seaweed, reached the age of twelve, thirteen, or fifteen years. He begins to sense the need for something which he cannot imagine, and he thinks: "It must be a rock bigger than these here, it must be a larger banana, a longer blade of grass, a fish more impressive than those which I see darting around in the water, a brighter star." What he senses within, because he is reaching puberty, is the need for something he does not know. He imagines that it may be like the reality surrounding him, yet different, *other*. And he absolutely cannot visualize a woman. The idea, quite simply, does not figure into his thinking. But if he were logical, he would say: "Behold, all these things that I want, bigger, more impressive, more, more ...; but no, it is some other thing that I want." So then he would have to conclude: "*There is* something in the universe, in reality, that corresponds to this want, my need, and it does not coincide with anything that I can grasp, and I don't know what it is." Why does he know that it exists? Because the existence of that thing is implied in the dynamic of his person. It is a reference made by something within himself, although it does not coincide with anything available to him, and he does not even know how to imagine it.

Just as a sign demonstrates the thing of which it is a sign, so the world in its impact with the human being functions a a sign, "demonstrates" *something else*, it demonstrates "God." A reality which can be experienced, whose adequate meaning, whose meaning conforms to human need, is something else. It is a *sign* of this something else.

It is important to emphasize the analogy between this phenomenon and the normal expression of human relationships. The human being experiences incomparable wholeness in companionship, in friendship, particularly between man and woman. Woman for man, and man for woman, or one person for another – these really constitute *other*. All of the rest can be assimilated or dominated by the human being, but the *you* – never. The *you* is inexhaustible, evident, not *demonstrable*. A human being cannot retrace the entire process which led to his present existence. Yet, man can know and experience fullness in no better way than before the *you*. Something distinct, by its nature different than me, something which is *other* fulfils me more than any experience of possession, domination, or assimilation.

THE DISCOVERY OF REASON

ILLUMINARE

Let us now try to highlight briefly the rational value of the sign's dynamic.

Reason is the need to understand existence, that is, the need for an adequate, total explanation of existence. This explanation cannot be found within the horizon of life's experience. No matter how much this horizon widens, this longing for an answer will remain: death makes incompleteness definitive.

Si Qilati

If reason is to be rescued, that is to say, if we want to be coherent with this energy that defines us, if we do not want to deny it, then its very dynamism forces us to affirm the exhaustive answer *beyond* the horizon of our life. The answer exists. It cries out through the entreaties that make up our being. But it cannot be defined by experience. It is there, but we do not know what it is.

Imagine that reason were a great mountain climber who scaled the highest summit on the globe and, once at the top, realized that the peak which he had just climbed was merely an infinitely small foothill leading to an enormous mountain whose beginning or end could not be seen. The summit of reason's conquest is the perception of an unknown unreachable presence, to which all human movement is destined, because it depends upon it. It is the idea of *mystery*.

We turn again to a poem by Clemente Rebora, *The Poplar Tree*, which expresses with clarity and intensity the same rational conclusion.

The stern poplar
quivers with its leaves in the wind;
the soul convulses with its pains
in the anxiety of thought:
from the trunk to the leafy limbs
all stretched to the sky:
the trunk of the mystery is anchored
and the trunk is rooted where
the truth lies.[6]

The meaning of the poem flows in the same stream as Gabriel Marcel's affirmation: "The mystery ... is that which makes things clear."[7] Mystery is not a limit to reason. Rather, it is reason's greatest discovery, the existence of something incommensurate in relation to itself.

To summarize: reason is the need to understand the existent, but because in life this is not possible, fidelity to reason forces us to admit the existence of something incomprehensible. This affirmation constitutes at once the sign of the smallness of our existence, and the sign of the incommensurable, infinite destiny of our existence, our reason, our being. Our intuition that mystery is implied by the very mechanism of our "I" is not an obstacle for reason; our "I" is not an osbstacle for reason, but a sign of its infinite openness.

Man's reason lives this dizzying condition: the explanation exists, but it is not within a person's grasp. It is there, but we do not know what it is like. In his *Germania*, Tacitus describes the idea of divinity as imagined by tribes he encountered: "Deorumque nominibus appellant sercretum illud, quod sola reverentia vident." "They call 'God' that hidden unattainable reality which they perceive only as something upon which their lives depend."[8]

Without this perspective, we deny reason in its essence, as the need for knowledge of the totality, and ultimately, as the very possibility for true knowledge.

There is a passage in Dostoevsky which describes a young aristocrat from Petersburg who has left his family to become a ship's captain.

He stays away from home for many years, sailing all over the world. When he finally returns, he enters into the salons of the noble class, where everyone is deriding religion and spouting out cynical and nihilistic discourses. These were the first rumblings of the German Aufklärung, which was to prepare the way for the political movements which would physically destroy the children and grandchildren of those aristocrats. This young man sits there, uneasy and silent, with his cup of tea in his hands and listens to these negative conversations. At a certain point, he stands up, pensively and spontaneously at the same time, and says: "But if God does not exist, am I still a ship's captain?"[9] If an ultimate link, a final explanation is not possible, if I cannot move out of this instant in order to reconnect myself with the whole (because the problem is precisely this, to "move out of" the instant, which means to reconnect yourself to the whole), then I can no longer establish any connection. I am stifled within the instant, and yesterday, the previous year, ten years ago, the long route leading to my captaincy is impossible to imagine, no sense can be made of it. Nothing means anything any more, because meaning is a connection that you establish when you step out of yourself, move out from the instant and place yourself in a relationship. And if you move out from your present moment, then the relationship flows like a torrent all the way to the end. "If God does not exist, am I still a ship's captain?" This is the concept of the sign in an existential and dramatic form.

Today's materialistic culture's cynicism impressively documents the meanness into which all that is human tends to decay immediately. Social life based upon cynicism leads to a total abolition of certainty, thus, also truth, justice, joy, and love. It reduces everything to a biological level.

Two objections could be made to all of this: First, it is not true that reason is the need for a total explanation, and, second, it is not true that life does not provide an exhaustive answer.

Let each person judge the truth of such objections.

Still, it would be useful to re-emphasize that the solution to the great question about life, which constitutes reason, is not an abstract hypothesis but an existential commitment, because this need is a lived experience.

OPENINGS

What we have just said explains why all of humanity's authentic religious traditions have referred to mystery, that is to say, spoken about God in negative terms: in-finite, im-mense, im-measurable, in-effable, that which cannot be spoken, unknown, that unknown god to which the Athenians had consecrated an altar. And even if certain words do seem positive – for example, omnipotent, omniscient, omnipresent – they are, in fact, negative from the standpoint of experience because they do not correspond to anything in our experience. They are positive only in a formal way and to understand them we must negate our own way of being powerful, or of knowing. Likewise, we use certain phrases: God is goodness, God is justice, God is beauty. They are starting points which, if multiplied, enrich the presentiment we have of this ultimate Object. But they cannot be definitions of this Object, because God is goodness, but He is not goodness in the way that we know goodness; God is love, but not love as we know it; God is person, but not as we are persons. However, these are not meaningless, purely nominalistic terms. Rather, they are expressions that intensify the way we relate to, draw closer to the Mystery. They are the openings to the Mystery.

12 The Adventure of Interpretation

No matter how obscure, enigmatic, nebulous, and veiled this "Other" may be, still it is undeniably the ultimate destination of the human impulse, the goal of the human dynamic.

Let us summarize our itinerary. Reason, which is to comprehend existence, to be coherent with its very nature, must admit that something incomprehensible, Something (of a *quid*) structurally *beyond* the possibility of understanding and measuring ("transcendent") exists:

> Everyone vaguely pictures in his mind
> > A good the heart may rest on, and is driven
> > By his desire to seek it and to find.
> >
> > ...
>
> Now, who art thou to be a judge, and scan
> > Truth from thy bench a thousand miles away,
> > With thy short sight that carries but a span?[1]

In the course of its adventure, reason reaches an ultimate pinnacle where it intuits the existence of this comprehensive explanation as something it cannot grasp on its own: this is mystery. It would not be reason if it did not imply the existence of this ultimate *quid*. Just as eyes on opening cannot but recognize colours and forms, so too the human person endowed with reason, which is set in motion by his impact with things, affirms the existence of of an ultimate, all-encompassing "because," an unknown *quid*, the *unknown God*. Do not let the word "God" confuse us because it is the term used, in universal religious language, to identify this absolute *quid*. In a billion centuries, whatever frontier the human person will have reached, still "that is not it," as Clemente Rebora again dramatically reveals to us in his poem, "Sandbags for the Eyes":

> Whatever you may say or do
>   there is a cry inside:
>   that is not why, that is not why!
> And thus everything refers back
>   to a secret question:
>   the act is a pretext.
>   ...
> In the imminence of God
>   life filches
>   ephemeral reserves,
>   while everyone clings
>   to some treasure of his which
>   shouts to him good-bye![2]

THE FACTOR OF FREEDOM BEFORE THE ULTIMATE ENIGMA

Now we must bring into play another essential element of the human being. Until now we have been concerned with reason, the consciousness factor. Now we need to confront the freedom factor.

The human person, as a free being, cannot be fulfilled, cannot reach his destiny except through freedom (see chapter 8). We have seen that to be free means the capacity to possess one's own meaning, reach one's realization according to a certain way that we, precisely, call freedom.

If I were forced to reach my destiny, I would not be able to be happy. It would be neither *my* happiness, nor *my* destiny. It is through my freedom that destiny, the end, the goal, the ultimate object becomes an answer given to me. Human fulfilment would not be human – would not be fulfilment – if it were not free. Now, if reaching destiny, fulfilment is to be free, freedom must "play a role" even in its *discovery*, for if the discovery of this destiny, this ultimate meaning were automatic, then this destiny would no longer be mine. The human person is responsible before his destiny; the way he attains it is his responsibility, the fruit of his freedom.

Freedom, then, has to do not only with our movement towards God as coherence of our lives, but, even before that, the very discovery of God. There are many scientists who, in deepening their experience as scientists, have discovered God; and there are many others who have thought to evade or eliminate God by means of their experience as scientists. In a similar way, many men and women of letters, through a profound perception of the human person's existence, have discovered God; and many others, through their attention to the human experience, have evaded or eliminated God. And, there are many philosophers who have arrived at God by means of their reflections; and many others who, through their reflections have excluded God. This, then, means that to recognize God is not solely a problem of science, aesthetic sensitivity, or philosophy as such. It is also a matter of freedom. One of the most noted neo-Marxists, Louis Althusser, recognized this when he said that between the existence of God and Marxism the problem is not one of reason, but option. Certainly, there is an option that is according to nature, which brings our reason to the fore. And there is an option that is against nature, and it obscures reason. However, after all is said and done, the option is decisive.

Let us reflect upon a comparison which will perhaps clarify my point. Standing in the half-light, you turn your back to the light and exclaim: "All is nothing. It is obscure, without sense." Then, you turn your back to the darkness and say: "The world is a vestibule of the light, the beginning of the light." The two positions are exclusively a matter of choice. Still, it is true that this is not the whole problem. Of the two positions, the one where the person turns his back to the light and exclaims, "All is shadow," or where the individual with his back towards the dark, says, "We are at the beginning of the light," one is right and the other is not. One of the two eliminates an almost imperceptible factor: indeed, if there is half-light, then there is light. This recalls what Jesus said several times in the Gospel: "I have performed many signs among you. Why do you not believe in me?" "You do not believe in me and turn against me in order that the prophecy be brought to pass, 'they hated me without cause'" (John 15: 22–5).

The human person, in fact, in his freedom, affirms what he has already secretly decided in the beginning. Freedom does not appear so much in the clamour of the choice. Rather, it is played out in the early, most subtle dawn of consciousness in its impact with the world. And here is the alternative in which man risks himself, even if *almost* unconsciously: either you face reality wide open, loyally, with the bright eyes of a child, calling a spade a spade, embracing its entire presence, even its meaning; either this, or you place yourself in front of reality, defend yourself against it, almost with your arms flung in front of your eyes to ward off unwelcomed and unexpected blows. You call reality to the tribunal of your opinion, and then potentially full of objections, having become too shrewd to accept its most gratuitous and surprising evidence and suggestions, you admit only what suits you. This is the profound choice we exercise daily before rain or sunshine, father and mother, before our breakfast, cars and buses and the people that ride with us, before our colleagues, school books, teachers, boyfriend, or girlfriend. The decision that I have described is made before reality, before all of it.

In making such a decision, it is clear that reasonableness or being wholly human, lies in an openness that calls a spade a spade. It is the attitude of the *poor* in spirit, those who, before reality, have absolutely nothing to defend who seize everything as it is, and follow the attraction of reality according to its total implications.

THE WORLD AS PARABLE

Freedom is exercised in that playing field called sign.

Let us remember that the world demonstrates the existence of the ultimate *quid*, the ultimate something, the mystery, by means of the "sign." The world "signals," demonstrates God, in the way that a sign indicates what it represents. How does freedom play itself out within this field? The sign is an event to *interpret* and freedom is exercised in the interpretation of the sign. Interpretation is the technique of the game, and freedom operates within this technique.

To cite a term from the Gospel (Matt. 13: 10ff), the world is like a parable. "Why do you speak in parables?" the apostles used to ask Christ. "The people do not understand you." Then as he would finish telling the parable, but while the crowd broke away, the apostles would run back to him and ask: "Explain the parable." Others would go away. The world is a parable. "I speak in parables so that seeing they may not see, and hearing they may not hear." In other words, "I speak in parables so that their freedom – what they have already decided in their hearts – might emerge."

If you are "moral," or another way of putting it, if you remain in the original attitude God gave you by creating you, that is to say, you are open to the real, then you understand, or at least you seek, that is, you ask. If, instead, you are not in that original position, that is to say, if you have been adulterated, corrupted, stalled by prejudice, then you are "immoral," and you cannot understand. And this is the supreme drama of human life.

The world, while it unveils, also "veils." The sign unveils, but at the same time it veils. And it is only a particular attention which allows us to sense, under or on the other side of this apparently inert fabric, the vibration of a living body lying behind it – not a mannequin, but a living body.

Suppose I were to go into a room where there was a beautiful painting on display. It has been placed in this room, designed so that the lights were hidden and would not interfere with a good view of the painting. I enter this room with you and say: "Hey, there aren't any lights in here." You answer: "Stop kidding around." I repeat "Look, there isn't any light." This time you become annoyed and reply: "Don't be eccentric, just let me look at the painting." And yet, I insist: "There isn't any light!" In the end, how would you answer me? Would you say: "Let's go and get the ladder and we'll see where the lights are hidden"? If this were necessary, then the both of us would be unreasonable. Indeed, why is there light? There is light because you can see the painting. If, there was no ladder to help us find out where the lights were, and I left saying: "No, there isn't any light!," I would be even more obviously unreasonable, stalled by a preconception. If one does not recognize the source of meaning and light which is the mystery of God the world would be, as we have already cited from Shakespeare, "A tale told by an idiot."[3]

The positivist is like someone who acts as if he were nearsighted, and within a centimetre of a painting, he fixes his gaze upon a certain point, exclaiming: "What a spot here!" And, because the painting is rather large, this person could go over the whole thing, centimetre by centimetre, exclaiming at every point, "What a spot here!" The painting would appear as a senseless collection of spots. But if he were to back off three metres, he would see the painting in its unity, in its entire perspective, and he would say: "Oh! Now I understand! How beautiful!" The positivist attitude is like viewing the world with a serious case of myopia.

Einstein was very far from this limited range of vision when he affirmed the ultimate enigmatic implication of reality, and thus also the value of the sign which, in a way that can never be eradicated, is at the heart of the world's vibration. "The fairest thing we can experience is the mysterious. It is the fundamental emotion which stands at the cradle of true art and true science." And, because of this, he was able to denounce that suffocating lack of consolation that comes from that myopia. "I answer, the man who regards his own life and that of his fellow creatures as meaningless is not merely unfortunate but almost disqualified for life."[4]

So it is that every serious empirical step and every precise scientific act must be pervaded by the call of the entire human horizon, "signalling" a higher, stronger, though enigmatic belonging. "The preoccupation for the human person and his destiny must always constitute the principal interest of all your technical efforts; among all of your diagrams and all of your equations, do not ever forget it."

13 An Education in Freedom

Demonstration through signs is the method that is adequate to the human being, it is characteristic of a personal life. The word, the gesture, what are they? They are signs. The love of a man and woman, friendship, and life together (*convivenza*) all use the sign as their instrument of communication. We have seen why: in this demonstrative method freedom plays itself out. It is respected. Freedom is played out in interpreting the sign.

EDUCATION IN FREEDOM AS RESPONSIBILITY

So here is the new step. The fundamental problem of the great adventure of this "sign" which is the world, is education in freedom because only through this education, this adventure, can destiny become evident. If reality refers the human being to something else, then education in freedom and responsibility are identical. Responsibility comes from the word "to respond." Education in responsibility is an education in responding to the call.

Of what does this education in freedom, that is to say, in responsibility, consist?

a) First of all, it implies an education in attention, for committed freedom does not necessarily imply attention because it is not automatically easy to be attentive. Preconception, no matter what its origin, impedes our attention. Preconception can mean the predomination of an interest and this leads to distraction, or the affirmation of a preformed idea and the rejection of a new message. It can also originate in concentrating one's sensitivity upon the pleasurable and thus becoming progressively insensitive towards details or nuances of a proposal, or handling things clumsily, briefly, and in a summary fashion, which becomes a crime when one treats a really serious problem.

Attention, above all, must take into account the totality of factors. How important is this dogged insistence on totality!

b) Second, an education in responsibility also means an education in the capacity for *acceptance*, because to welcome a proposal in its integrity is not automatic either.

An education that forms attentiveness and acceptance, marked by a sensitivity towards all of the factors in play, teaches one to open doors, perhaps already prematurely closed, even if for a perfectly good reason: for at any hour whatsoever, even at night, the substance of reality might knock at the door.

An education in attention and acceptance assures the correct fundamental attitude in front of reality – wide open, free, and without presumption, which calls reality up to face our own verdict, an attitude that does not judge reality on the basis of preconception. To summarize, educating one's freedom to attentiveness, that is, to be wide open toward the totality of factors at play, and educating it to acceptance, that is, to the conscious embrace of what it finds before it is the fundamental issue of the human journey.

AN EDUCATION IN LEARNING HOW TO ASK

An education in freedom, necessary for an adequate interpretation of that sign that is existence, the world, must train the individual to assume a correct attitude in front of reality. What is the proper attitude? It is to remain in the original position in which nature places the human being. And such an original attitude, a native stamp, impressed upon the person by nature, is expectation which manifests itself in the form of asking.

In a child, this is present as curiosity: expectation and asking. In the adult it is expectation and searching. It must be a real quest: a false one flings questions against reality without expecting an answer. Searching for the sake of searching is to seek willingly a false answer.

A real search always implies a positive answer as an ultimate hypothesis: otherwise one would not search. Thus, if reality provokes us, then an education in freedom must teach one to respond to pro-vocation. It is an education in "hungering" and "thirsting" which makes us attentive to the many solicitations emerging from our confrontation with the totality of the real, ready to accept any valuable aspect, that is, any serious promise to the essential need of our being. Blessed are those who hunger and thirst. Contrarily, cursed are those who do not hunger and thirst, who already know, who expect nothing. Cursed are the satisfied for whom reality, at best, is a pure pretext for making a commotion, and who do not expect anything really new from it.

The correct attitude, the one the human being is placed in by nature for his confrontation with the real, is positive. Curiosity is the most immediately mechanical manifestation of this profound attention which nature awakens in the human person before the cosmos. What does this original curiosity mean? Curiosity in either a child or an adult is an open disposition, full of positive affirmation, nothing other than an original sympathy with being, with reality, a general working hypothesis, which nature uses to thrust the human being towards a universal comparison. This sympathy with reality is the general working hypothesis, the premise for any action, any activity whatsoever.

The position of doubt makes us incapable of action. I remember reading in a newspaper one time about a certain school established in the United States. Its purpose was to form a special capacity for invention in super-intelligent children. In other words, it was a school for educating geniuses, because coming up with new inventions is an act of genius. This entire school was designed to teach children to approach problems with a positive hypothesis. The worst thing in the world is to place oneself in front of reality with a hypothesis, not necessarily negative, but simply suspended. In such a situation, one no longer advances.

This observation is simple enough: if one begins with a negative hypothesis, then even if there is something there to find, it will not be found; if, on the other hand, one starts out with a positive hypothesis, then if there is something there, it will be found, and, if not, then it will not.

In that particularly beautiful novel by Graham Greene, *The End of the Affair,*[1] there is a very significant episode. The protagonist is a free thinker, an anarchist writer in London. He visits a friend whose wife has died and there he finds a priest, the confessor of the dead woman. Seeing him there, the protagonist, in a veritable hailstorm of words that seems to submerge the priest, pours out all of his anger towards religion, deriding God, miracles, etc. But the priest, taking advantage of a brief pause where the speaker catches his breath, says something like this: "But, at this point I would have to say that it seems to me that I am a freer thinker than you! Because it seems to me freer thinking to admit all possibilities, rather than to preclude any." The positive hypothesis is an option, a choice. An education in freedom must teach the individual to opt for the positive beginning.

There exists nothing more pathological and unproductive than systematic doubt. I remember a young friend who, at a certain point during his high school years, precisely due to the problem of religion, suffered from a terrible nervous breakdown. He doubted everything. He seemed to be the very incarnation of a certain character in the works of Luigi Pirandello. His father brought him to a psychiatrist who took him into a room where there was a bald man. The boy could see the man only from behind. The man, with a flashlight in hand, was searching for something, running the light along the line where the floor meets the wall. The doctor called the man by name. Although the man did not turn his head, he stopped his activity. When the doctor, again calling him by name, asked him: "What are you looking for?" the man answered with his first and last names. A new Diogenes, he was looking for himself. Well, I think that my friend recovered, also thanks to this shock.

An education in freedom is an education in positiveness before the real, in cultivating a capacity for certainty. All of these "buts, ifs, howevers, and perhaps," are words used to help weaken the positive way the "I" relates to reality. They are a defensive volley of gunfire, a smokescreen protecting a person's retreat from a commitment to reality itself.

THE EXPERIENCE OF RISK

Why is it so difficult for man to read that mysterious name suggested, signalled by the entire call to him from the real, to identify the existence of God, of mystery, the meaning that lies beyond himself? Where precisely is the problem?

It is useful here to observe again how nature makes it absolutely easy for man to perceive those things most essential for living. Of these, the most necessary is the intuition of the existence of the reason why, of meaning, the existence of God. In his *Apologia Pro Vita Sua*,[2] the great John Henry Newman remembers that at fifteen years of age he was struck, as if by a lightning bolt, with the intuition that there were "only two and two only absolute and luminously self-evident beings: myself and my Creator." The supreme ease in accepting the existence of God is identified with the immediateness of perceiving the existence of the self. Indeed, as we have seen, God is the most immediate implication of self-consciousness. If the world is viewed in a humane manner, the most obvious and unyielding implication is the presentiment and the intuition of the existence of an adequate meaning, of what we call God, that mysterious "x," that "sublime neutral."

In view of this, then, I would like to contribute to the discovery of the root of man's difficulty in admitting the existence of God.

The inevitable consequence of a relationship with God, mediated by the phenomenon of the sign, is what I call the experience of risk. Interpreting the sign is like crossing a narrow strait, as when Ulysses sailed the ocean beyond the Pillars of Hercules. Risk is not a gesture or an action without adequate reasons, because then it would not be a risk – it would be irrationality. Risk is something else.

I understood this concept well when, by chance, many years after the fact, I remembered an episode from my childhood. I was always asking to be taken along on those high dangerous trails that require hikers to climb linked together by a rope. But they always answered me saying, "You are too small." Then one day they said to me, "If you pass your exams next June, we will take you for your first rope climb." And so it happened. Ahead of me was the guide, then I, and, following me, were two men. We had climbed beyond the half-way point of the trail when, at a certain moment, I saw the guide make a small jump. Three or four metres behind him, nervously holding the rope in my hand, I heard the guide say, "All right now, jump!" I found myself on a ledge with another one commencing about a metre beyond it, and beneath me was a deep ravine. I leapt back and grabbed onto a large outcropping of rock. Three grown men were unable to budge me from that position. I remember the voices repeating to me, "Don't be afraid, we're here with you!" And I was saying to myself, "You're stupid, they'll carry you." And, although I kept saying this to myself, I could not bring myself to let go of that rock.

This exceptional panic led me to understand, many years later, the experience of risk. It was not the lack of reasons that prevented me from jumping. I had many reasons not to be afraid, but it was as if they were written on the air, leaving me unaffected. It is analogous to a situation where a person says, "Yes you are right, but I am not persuaded." There is a hiatus, an abyss, a void between the intuition of truth, of being – given by reason – and the will, a disassociation between reason, the perception of being, and will, which is affectivity, that is to say, the energy of adhesion to being (Christianity would point out in this experience a wound produced by "original sin"). Because of this, one sees the reasons, but still does not move, that is to say, lacks the energy to be coherent. We are not referring to coherent here in the ethical sense of consequential behaviour, but in its theoretical aspect as intellectually adhering to the truth, which reasons let one glimpse. It is this coherence that initiates the human being's unity. Coherence is the energy with which man takes hold of himself and adheres, "fastens on" to what reason lets him see. On the contrary, a break occurs between reason and affectivity, between reason and will: this is the experience of risk.

This is no abstract hypothesis. It is something very concrete. There could be a man, for example, who, for seven years, had been engaged to a woman and still cannot decide whether or not to marry her. This is not because he is devious. He cannot decide because he is continually saying to himself: "And then ... ; and if ... ; what if ... ; and how can I be sure ... ?" That man would not be experiencing any sense of risk if he were not facing the decision of marriage. Indeed, when does the sense of risk penetrate the person? It does so to the extent that the object involves the meaning of one's own existence, and, the more this is so, the greater the sense of this irrational division.

I have given the example of the man who is to be married. Yet, it is evident that the question of life's total meaning, of the existence of God, strikes much deeper than this. Here is a serious division between the energy of adhering to being, and reason as the discovery of being. Here, the covering fire of the "buts," "ifs," and "maybes," as I was saying before, protects our retreat from our commitment to the mystery. This is the supreme immorality: immorality in front of one's own destiny.

Let us return to my childhood memory. How might I have been able to let go of my death grip on that ledge of rock? Only with an enormous amount of will power. But I did not have this will power which, in any case was not the answer. It would have been too difficult in this kind of situation to muster such pure and strong energy. For only an enormous amount of will power could have made me submit to reasons that seem abstract.

Only a great deal of will power might enable an individual to overcome a fear of affirming being. And, here then lies the true definition of the experience of risk: a strange fear of affirming being; strange because it is extraneous to, it contradicts our nature. The more something involves the meaning of living, the more we fear affirming it. And while this fear could be conquered by the effort of the will, that is, by the force of freedom, it is highly improbable.

Nature has a method which manages to give us this energy of freedom, enabling us to overcome, pass through the fear aroused by risk, to conquer the abyss of the "buts," "ifs," and "howevers." This is the *communital* phenomenon.

A child runs down a hallway, pushes open with his little hands the door, which is always open, to an unlit room. Frightened, he turns back. His mother arrives and leads him by the hand. With his hand in his mother's, the child will go into any unlit room in the world. Only the communital dimension renders the human being sufficiently capable of overcoming the experience of risk.

I remember my school days, when a class let itself be influenced by a philosophy or history teacher and the majority of the class would be against the religious fact, even the two or three students more sensitive to religion would be intimidated. However, in a class where the common religious conviction of a few students was felt, then the teacher, despite all of his dialectic and intimidation, could not destroy a general atmosphere open to the religious problem.

The communital dimension does not replace freedom, personal energy, and decision. Rather, it is the condition for their affirmation. If, for example, I place the seed of a beech tree on a table, it will not develop into anything, even after a thousand years (assuming that everything remains the same). If, on the other hand, I take this seed and plant it in the ground, then it eventually becomes a tree. Now the humus does not replace the irreducible energy, the incommunicable "personality" of the seed. Rather, the humus is the condition needed for the seed to grow.

The community is the dimension and condition necessary for the human seed to bear fruit. For this reason, we can say that the true, the most intelligent persecution, is not the one employed by Nero and his amphitheatre of wild beasts or the concentration camp. The most ferocious persecution is the modern state's attempt to block the expression of the communital dimension of the religious phenomenon. As far as the state is concerned, a person can, in conscience, believe what he likes, as long as this faith does not imply that all believers are one, and therefore, have the right to live and express this reality. To obstruct communital expression is like cutting off the roots that nourish the plant: the plant soon dies.

The real drama of the relation between the human being and God, through that sign which is the cosmos, through that sign which is experience, does not lie in the fragility of the reasons, because the entire world is one great reason and there does not exist one human outlook upon reality which does not feel the provocation of this perspective which supercedes it. The real drama lies in the will which must adhere to this overwhelming evidence, and the dramatic quality is defined by what I call risk. The human being undergoes the experience of risk in the following manner: despite reasons encouraging him to act, an individual is unable to do so. It is as if he were paralyzed, needed an extra dose of energy and will, of the energy of freedom, because freedom is the capacity to adhere to being.

An individual who lives out his communital dimension experiences a more adequate energy of freedom. It is in this sense then that we can understand Chesterton's paradox that says: "... two is not twice one; two is two thousand times one"[3] and also appreciate the genius of Christ who identified his religious experience with the Church: "There where two or three are gathered in my name, there also shall I be" (Matt. 18:20).

14 Reason's Energy Seeks to Penetrate the Unknown

Fundamentally, we have defined reason as a relationship with the infinite that reveals itself as the need for a total explanation. Reason's highest achievement is the intuition that an explanation exists exceeding the measure of reason itself. Using a prior play on words, reason, precisely as the need to comprehend existence, is forced by its very nature to admit the existence of something incomprehensible. Now, when reason becomes conscious of itself down to its core and discovers that it ultimately realizes its nature by intuiting the unreachable, the mystery, it does not cease to be a need for knowledge.

REASON'S DRIVING FORCE

Once this is discovered, reason yearns to know the unknown. The life of reason is the will to penetrate the unknown (like Dante's Ulysses), to pass beyond the Pillars of Hercules, the symbol of the continuous and structural limit existence imposes on this desire.[1] Even more, in fact, it is precisely the endeavour to penetrate this unknown, that defines reason's energy. As we have indicated, in the Acts of the Apostles, St Paul, speaking before the "philosophers" who habitually met together at the Areopagus of Athens, said:

The God who has made the world and all that it holds, who is Lord of heaven and of earth, does not dwell in the temples built by human hands, nor is he served by human hands as though he had need of something, for it is he who gives life and breath and everything to all. He created all nations from one people, so that they might inhabit the whole face of the earth. It is he who set limits to their epochs and fixed the boundaries of their regions, so that they may seek out God, that they may one day come to find him, going on gropingly, although he is not far from any one of us. In him, in fact, we live, move and have our being, and even one of your own poets has said, "For we are all of us his people."[2]

All of the movement of humanity, all of the endeavour of this "laborious force which wearies us by keeping us in motion,"[3] is the knowledge of God. The immense effort expended in searching is summed up in the expression "the movement of peoples." To discover, to enter into the mystery that underpins the reality that appears before us – what we see and touch – this is reason's motivation, its driving force.

It is this relationship with that "beyond," which ensures the adventure of the here and now. Otherwise, boredom dominates – a boredom which is the origin of either the elusive and evasive presumption or censorious desperation. Only the relationship with the "beyond" makes the adventure of life possible. The will to penetrate the beyond gives man the energy to seize the here and now.

The ancient myth closest to today's mentality has found its most powerful expression on Christian soil; this is the myth of Ulysses. In no other place or time, not in any version of ancient literature, has this myth found such an expressive force as in the work of Dante Alighieri. None whatsoever.

Ulysses is the intelligent man who would measure all things with his own acumen. He is relentlessly curious, the master of the *Mare Nostrum* (the Mediterranean). Imagine this man, with all of his sailors on his boat – wandering from Ithaca to Lybia, from Lybia to Sicily, from Sicily to Sardinia, from Sardinia to the Balearics – measuring and governing the entire *Mare Nostrum,* sailing over every inch, its length and its width. Man is the measure of all things. But, once he arrives at the Pillars of Hercules, he confronts a common belief that all wisdom, that is, the certain measure of all that is real, is no longer possible. Beyond the Pillars of Hercules, nothing is reliable any longer – all is emptiness and madness. And just as he who ventures beyond this point is a dreamer who will never again have any certainty, so beyond the confines of experience – positivistically understood – there is only fantasy or at least the impossibility of certainty.

But he, Ulysses, precisely because of that same "stature" that had driven him all over the *Mare Nostrum,* felt not only that the Pillars of Hercules were not the end, but they were, in fact, the moment of the unleashing of his true nature. And so he smashed to smithereens this wisdom and went on. He did not make a mistake in doing so: to venture forward was in his nature as a man, and, in making this decision, he truly felt like a man. Ulysses exemplifies this struggle between the human, the religious sense, and the inhuman, the positivist position which marks the entire modern mentality. The latter would say: "My boy, the only sure thing is what you measure and verify scientifically, with experimentation. Beyond this is useless fantasy, madness, and imaginative assertions."

But beyond the *Mare Nostrum*, what we can possess, govern, and measure, what is there? Beyond is the ocean of meaning. It is in daring to go beyond the Pillars of Hercules – this extreme limit erected by false wisdom, and that oppressive security – and to advance into the enigma of meaning that one really begins to feel like a human being. Reality in its impact with the human heart draws out the dynamic that the Pillars of Hercules evoked in the heart of Ulysses and his companions, their faces taut with desire for "other." For those anxious faces and those hearts full of longing, the Pillars of Hercules were not a boundary, but an invitation, a sign, something which recalls one beyond. No, the error of Ulysses and his helmsmen was not that they continued their journey!

But there is a text even greater, even more expressive of this existential position of human reason than Dante's Ulysses – it is in the Bible (Gen. 32:23–33), when Jacob returns home from exile, that is to say, from the dispersion or a foreign reality. He reaches the river at twilight, and darkness is rapidly descending. Already the herds, servants, children, and women have passed by. By the time it is his turn to wade the ford, it is completely dark, but Jacob wants to continue on. But before he sets foot in the water, he senses an obstacle in front of him. A person confronts him and tries to prevent him from crossing. Jacob cannot see this person's face but, with all of his strength, he starts to wrestle with him in a match that will last the entire night. Finally at the first rays of dawn, the strange person manages to inflict such a blow on Jacob's hip that from then on, for the rest of his life, Jacob will be lame. But at the same moment, the strange individual says to Jacob, "You are indeed great. You shall no longer be spoken of as Jacob, but as Israel which means 'I have wrestled with God.'" This is the stature of the human being in Judeo-Christian revelation. Life, the human being is a struggle, that is to say a tension, a relation "in darkness" with the beyond; a struggle without seeing the face of the other. He who realizes this about himself goes among others as lame, singled out. He is no longer like the others. He is marked.

A VERTIGINOUS POSITION

If this is the existential position of reason, then it is easy enough to see how it can be dizzying. By law, by my life's directive, I must hang suspended, moment by moment, upon a will that I do not know. This would be the only rational position. The Bible (Ps. 123:2) would say "... like the eyes of a servant attentively looking for the nod of the master ... " For one's whole life, the true moral law would be that of waiting for the nod of this unknown "lord," attentive to the signs of a will that would appear to us through pure, immediate circumstance.

I repeat: man, the human being's rational life would have to be suspended on the instant, suspended in every moment upon this sign, apparently so fickle, so haphazard, yet the circumstances through which the unknown "lord" drags me, provokes me toward his design. I would have to say "yes" to every instant without seeing anything, simply adhering to the pressures of the occasions. It is a dizzying position.

REASON'S IMPATIENCE

The human being's reason, in its impassioned desire, in its claim to understand the supreme meaning upon which all of its acts depend, is pushed by what the Bible reveals as "an excessive attachment to self" (the identical psychological formula is given as: "self love"), to say: "All right I understand: the mystery *is* this." In other words, *existentially*, because reason – the need to know, to comprehend – penetrates everything, it, therefore, also claims to penetrate the unknown, upon which everything, every breath and heartbeat, moment by moment, depends. Reason is impatient. It cannot bear to adhere to the single unique sign that is the means for following the Unknown. This sign, which is the chain of circumstances, is so obtuse, so dark, so opaque, so accidental that to pursue it is like placing yourself at the mercy of a river's currents that toss you here and there.

In its existential situation, reason can stave off this vertigo at first. But eventually it will give in. This dizziness lies in the prematurity, the impatience which leads it to claim: "I understand, life's meaning is this." All of these affirmations – "the meaning of the world *is* this, the sense of being human *is* this, history's ultimate destiny *is* this" – in all of their diversity and multiplicity are all testimonies to that *giving in*.

A DISTORTING POINT OF VIEW

But when the human being's reason affirms that, "My life's meaning is ... " "The meaning of the world is ... " "The meaning of history is ..." then it inevitably goes on to define what this *is:* it is the blood of the Aryan race, the struggle of the proletariat, the competition for economic supremacy, etc. Every time a definition is completed, it will inevitably begin from a certain point of view. Another way of saying this would be: if the human being claims to define the total meaning, he can only end up exalting his own point of view, one point of view. He cannot avoid claiming *totality for a particular,* inflating a detail to define the whole. This position must attempt to make every aspect of reality fit into its own perspective. And, since he is only dealing with a detail, his attempt to make everything fit into it cannot escape denying or forgetting something; it cannot help reducing, negating, and repudiating the entire, complex face of reality. In this way, the religious sense, or reason as the affirmation of an ultimate meaning, is corrupted, degraded to the point where the person identifies it with something of his own choosing, necessarily within the ambit of his own experience. This is a choice that distorts the real face of one's whole life because everything will be widened or shrunken, exalted or forgotten, praised or shunted aside according to the extent of the involvement with the chosen point of view, the selected factor.

Now where does the "pathos" of this attitude lie? It lies in the fact that the religious sense, that is the human being's nature in its ultimate stature, will identify the whole of life's meaning with something comprehensible to it. And here is the root of the error: "with something comprehensible to it." Reason is the need to comprehend. And, because of this, it experiences dizziness before the intuition of the unknown, the mystery, and, almost unwittingly, it slips. Its outlook becomes degraded, and, focusing upon one aspect among many in its existence, one factor among all of the complex of factors in its experience, it says: "This is the meaning."

Reason intuits the mystery, the incommensurability of the total meaning with its possibility of knowing by the very fact that it is put into motion. That is the nature of reason. Yet, existentially, reason does not hold up or sustain its original impetus. It falls out of the true arc of its flight, immediately losing altitude. It degrades the object by identifying it with itself, with something it fully comprehends, that is, within the confines of its experience, because experience is the horizon of the comprehensible.

If I have chosen something within my experience of what is comprehensible, then I have exalted a particular to explain everything.

We have said that the real problem basic to this entire discussion is to understand what reason is: is it the ambit of the real or an opening upon the real? However, our experience shows us that reason is like an eye opened widely upon reality, a passageway into being, which we never stop entering and, which, by its nature, overflows its rim. This is why the total meaning is mystery.

The decadence, the degradation we have referred to, the deterioration of reason's flight path by a kind of gravitational force, lies in the claim that reason can measure the real, identify, and thus define, what the meaning of everything should be. In the final analysis, what does it mean to claim to define the meaning of everything? It means to claim to be the measure of everything, or, in other words, it means to *claim to be God.*

IDOLS

The first pages of the Bible really provide the clearest explanation. Genesis teaches us that it is not true that there is something that you cannot ("eat," in biblical language) measure; and if you decide to do it, if you set out on this adventure, then "you will know good from evil, like God." This is the temptation of original sin. The human being becomes the measure of all things. The Bible also precisely names the *particular* that reason identifies as the total meaning of life and the existence of all things. It refers to this *particular* as an *idol,* as something which seems to be God, has the mask of God, but is not.

The lie of the idol is defined by St Paul in the *Letter to the Romans* (1:22–31):

They claimed to be wise, but turned into fools instead; they exchanged the glory of the immortal God for images representing mortal man, birds, beasts and snakes. In consequence, God delivered them up in their lusts to unclean practices; they engaged in the mutual degradation of their bodies, these men who exchanged the truth of God for a lie and worshipped and served the creature rather than the creator – blessed be he forever, amen! God therefore delivered them up to disgraceful passions. Their women exchanged natural intercourse for unnatural, and the men gave up natural intercourse with women and burned with lust for one another. Men did shameful things with men and thus received in their own persons the penalty for their perversity. They did not see fit to acknowledge God, so God delivered them up to their own depraved senses to do what is unseemly. They are filled with every kind of wickedness: maliciousness, greed, ill will, envy, murder, bickering, deceit, craftiness. They are gossips and slanderers, they hate God, are insolent, haughty, boastful, ingenious in their wrongdoing and rebellious toward their parents. One sees in them men without conscience, without loyalty, without affection, without pity. They know God's just decree that all who do such things deserve death; yet they not only do them but approve them in others.[4]

In this passage, St Paul describes not only the genesis of the idol, but also the resulting corruption of human truth. The more one *tries* to explain everything with an idol, the more one understands that it is simply not sufficient: "They have eyes, but do not see, have ears and do not hear, have hands and do not touch," (Ps. 153:15–17). In

138 The Religious Sense

other words, they do not keep their promises or fulfil their claim that they provide a total answer. Mystery, on the other hand, to the extent that it is recognized, tends to determine life, rendering the terrible list, enumerated by St Paul, mute, empty. Idols, to the extent that they are exalted, diminish what is human. Idolatry is the abolition of the person, of human responsibility, to the point where the individual blames, not himself for misfortunes, but structures. The idol obscures the horizon of our gaze and alters the form of things. So then, as Eliot prophetically writes:

> They constantly try to escape
> From the darkness outside and within
> By dreaming of systems so perfect that no one will need to be good.
> But the man that is will shadow
> The man that pretends to be.[5]

A CONSEQUENCE

There is an impressive corollary to all of this. Hitler had his idol, upon which he hoped to build a life in this world for a better humanity. But this construction of his, which sought to embrace everything, found itself, at a certain point, in conflict with the dynamism of Lenin's and Stalin's projects. So then what? By its very nature, the ideology built upon the idol is all-encompassing. Otherwise it would not be able to claim to be convincing. So, if we have two ideologies, both all-encompassing, they cannot avoid generating a total conflict. This explains why, for the Bible, the idol is the origin of violence as a system of relationships, the origin of war.

One of Aesop's fables is very pertinent to our discussion. This particular of experience that is chosen for ideological reasons as the total explanation is like Aesop's frog who puffs itself up in order to become an ox, puffing and puffing until it explodes. This is the symbol of war's violence.

DYNAMICS OF THE IDENTIFICATION OF THE IDOL

We can make another important observation. As we have seen, the human person will identify God with the idol by choosing something which he himself *understands*. This is original sin, the claim of being able to identify the total meaning with something comprehensible. It is as if he were to maintain that "what exists is demonstrable, while that which cannot be demonstrated by man does not exist." But, as we have already said, the original passage, the most important step cannot be taken by man – he cannot bring things into being. He can manipulate what exists, but he cannot cause things to "be."

In this dynamic of identifying an idol, a person selects the thing he admires most, or better yet, the thing that impresses him the most. He could even identify the divine with a social principle. An example of this "barbaric" state, right smack in the middle of the twentieth century, is the Nazi myth which identified the meaning of history with the blood of the German race.

A well-known Italian priest, the late Father Carlo Gnocchi, having just returned from a battlefield in Russia in World War II, told a group of friends one evening about something that happened to him there. While the Germans were retreating he entered an encampment of very young German officers. He wore a black cross which identified him as a military chaplain. Initially they ridiculed him, and then confronted him angrily. At one point, one of these officers leapt to his feet and, extending his arm towards the photograph of Hitler, hanging on the wall, cried: "This is our Christ." And it was true, he was their Christ. In the same way, for coherent Marxists, the proletariat is their Christ, whose supreme expression is the party head.

The human being cannot avoid this alternative: either he is the slave of men or a subject, dependent upon God.

This is the truly barbaric oppression: the violence of social forces, when seen as the bearer of ultimate meaning, is always right. Consequently, if you kill in the name of these social forces it is good (as we have seen in the tragedy of Vietnam and Cambodia). What their own partners do is democracy, while if others do it, then it is a crime.

Let us make this final observation: man, from time immemorial, as he matures in history, tends to identify god, that is the meaning of the world, based on a particular aspect of his own self. I have already noted that in our disquiet, this game, the game of the idol, repeats itself, contradicting itself one hundred times a day. The idol can never bring about unity or totality without forgetting or denying something!

CONCLUSION

The world is a sign. Reality calls us on to another reality. Reason, in order to be faithful to its nature and to the nature of such a calling, is forced to admit the existence of something else underpinning, explaining everything.

By nature, the human being intuits the Beyond. However, because of an existential condition, he does not hold up, he falls. Intuition is like an impulse falling off due to some sad and malignant force of gravity. Ulysses and his men were mad not because they sailed on past the Pillars of Hercules, but because they claimed to identify the meaning, that is, to sail the ocean beyond the Pillars, with the very means they used to sail the "measurable" shores of the *Mare Nostrum*.

Reality is a sign, and it awakens our religious sense. But it is a suggestion that is misinterpreted. Existentially, the human being is driven to interpret it poorly; that is to say, prematurely, with impatience. The intuition of our relationship with mystery becomes degraded into presumption.

For this reason, St Thomas Aquinas says at the beginning of his *Summa Theologiae*:

The truth concerning God that reason is able to attain is accomplished only by a very few, and this only after much time and not without the inclusion of error. On the other hand, the entire salvation of the human being depends upon the knowledge of this truth, since this salvation is in God. In order to render this salvation more universal and more certain, it would have thus been necessary to teach men this divine truth with a divine revelation.[6]

This is the most synthetic description of the existential situation of humanity's religious sense. The human religious genius has cried out, in so many ways, to be liberated from this inextricable captivity of impotence and error. Perhaps the most powerful expression of this condition is to be found in Plato's *Phaedo:*

Well spoken, said Simmias. I will tell you my difficulty, and then Cebes will say why he does not accept what was said. I believe, as perhaps you do, that precise knowledge on that subject is impossible or extremely difficult in our present life, but that it surely shows a very poor spirit not to examine thoroughly what is said about it, and to desist before one is exhausted by an all-round investigation. One should achieve one of these things: learn the truth about these things or find it for oneself, or, if that is impossible, adopt the best and most irrefutable of men's theories, and, borne upon this, sail through the dangers of life as upon a raft, unless someone should make that journey safer and less risky upon a firmer vessel of some divine doctrine.[7]

The Hypothesis of Revelation: Conditions For Its Acceptability

Our nature is need for truth and fulfilment, or, in other words, happiness. All human movement, whatever it might be, is dictated by this urgency that constitutes us. But this desire, having reached the extreme borders of our life experience, still does not find what it has been searching for: at the utmost frontier of its lived territory, this urgent need of ours still has not found its answer. And the apparent wall of death clearly testifies to the reality of this observation.

It is here where the question springs up. Our reason, our humanity, by the force of its nature, in order not to suppress itself, intuits the answer implied by its own dynamism – an answer which exists by the very fact that the need exists. It would be necessary to choose total irrationality, something completely contrary to our nature that would stifle the impulse by which our nature reaches the intuition that this ultimate meaning, this total dependence has a term of reference – even if it is (and we will use here a dramatic word) "desperately" beyond. It lies beyond, "trans," it is "transcendent," "absolute," tied neither to time and space, nor any of the capacities at our disposal that belong to reason, fantasy, or imagination.

The realization of the existence of this supreme unknown, upon which all history and the world depends, is reason's pinnacle and its vertigo. This means that, ideally, a human being who fulfils his true capacity, his by nature – with all of his will for life, his affection for the real – ought to be at the mercy of, hanging on moment by moment, to this unreachable, indecipherable, ineffable, absolute Unknown. How does this Unknown reveal its will to the human being? How does it communicate its intelligent plan that guarantees the meaning of everything? It speaks through apparently fortuitous circumstances, the banal conditions that determine the human being's every instant.

What a paradox! In order to follow the absolute light of meaning, one would have to be obedient, like one navigating in dense fog, moment by moment, obeying the very thing that is most apparently irrational, that is to say, absurdly shifting circumstances, subject to the wind of time.

One needs great courage. Like Jacob, of whom we have spoken, who spent the entire night, the time of existence, struggling with this unseizable, indecipherable, faceless Presence. Here man feels his head spin.

And so history is like a great film all about this human decline, although pervaded by the ideal drive that provokes it. Man relapses into the terms of his own experience, the horizon of his own existence. And since the human being cannot live five minutes without affirming in some way some ultimate "something" that makes those five minutes worth living, the inexorable and urgent need for a meaning generates a kind of anxiety, a fear, or terror; and in terror the human person finds himself helpless. It is as if the individual grasps on to his existentiality in an excessive way – like someone who is drowning and hysterically grabs hold of whomever is near. Filled with terror, he is pushed into identifying the absolute, the sure and solid, with something within what the realm of his own experience, which ultimately makes life worth living, with some facet, the most reassuring aspect of his existence. In this way the god becomes idol.

I would like to add that the person who recognizes the mystery as mystery, but then establishes his own route, is also subject to this fall, for, in doing this, he identifies the ultimate end point.

In short, it is historically inevitable that man, at a certain point, will identify the absolute with one of his own images. In this way, the history of human thought extensively documents this fall that occurs in either an explicit or implicit way, theorized or practised, established in a theory or lived in a moment, or a particular hour.

Following the example of the Bible, we have already discussed all of the consequences of this fall: life as violence and corruption. In fact, the relationships, through which man attempts to take on the entire universe (as a vast extension of his body), the relationships become the means by which he throws himself into the search for and the possession of the "you," or, in other words, the possession of others, other persons; all this is approached according to one's own point of view, to one's own measure, and not in a measure that derives from a connection with the absolute. In this way, the human person mutilates himself, others, the things around him. He creates abnormal images with schizophrenic forms. "Oh, unhappy me," St Paul would say, "who will free me from this deadly situation?" (Rom. 7:24).

The longing for a "redemption," for a sure route to cross the sea of meaning, had been prophetically voiced four centuries before Christ, in Plato's *Phaedo*. We have already seen this. At the extremity of life's experience, at the edge of this passionate and hard-won conscious-ness of existence, in spite of man himself, this cry of the truest humanity breaks out as an entreaty, a begging. And then emerges the great hypothesis: "unless someone take this passage on a more solid craft, that is to say, with the help of a revealed word of God."

Properly speaking, this is called hypothesis of *revelation*. The word revelation has a broader and more generic sense: the world, by its very structure, is this revelation of God, of mystery. Reality is a sign, and, when human consciousness interprets this sign, it understands the existence of mystery. In this sense, then the world by its very structure is the revelation of God. And human beings hear the pre-sence of a "Beyond" by interpreting the dynamic structure of their relationship with things.

In the proper sense of the word, "revelation" does not signify the outcome of man's *interpretation* of reality, human nature in search of its meaning. Rather, revelation means a possibly real *fact*, an historical event, which the human person may or may not recognize. In fact, neither Judas, nor the majority of those who saw it, recognized it.

However, that God, in some way, should enter into human history as a factor inside history, not just as some ultimate shore, beyond appearances that man must overcome, but as a presence within history that speaks as a friend, a father, a mother – Plato's *Phaedo* aspired to this kind of revelation.

This is the exceptional hypothesis, revelation in the strict sense of the word: that the mystery reveals itself through a factor of history with which, as in the case of Christianity, it identifies itself. In Eliot's words:

Men's curiosity searches past and future
And clings to that dimension. But to apprehend
The point of intersection of the timeless
With time, is an occupation for the saint ...
No occupation either, but something given
And taken, in a lifetime's death in love,
Ardour and selflessness and self-surrender.[1]

A similar hypothesis is *first of all possible*. To Mary who asked, "How is it possible?" the Angel answered, "For God nothing is impossible"

(Luke 1:34–7). To deny that this hypothesis is possible, is the ultimate and extreme form of idolatry, reason's most drastic attempt to impose on God its own image of Him. Because if God is the mystery, how can one dictate to Him what He can and cannot do?

In the *second* place, this hypothesis is extremely *convenient* – it responds to human desire, adapts itself to the human being's heart and nature. It is the answer to our normally unconscious expectancy, the height of con-venience ("venience," from the Latin verb meaning "to come").

In such a hypothesis, God certainly does not suppress the human being's freedom to act, but makes it possible, because man's error and fatigue limit his operative freedom. Perhaps this example will illustrate my point. One time, as a boy, I got lost in a large wood. I ran for an hour and a half or two, going further into the thick of the forest without finding any way out. And, as the sun was setting, I became terrified, and so I began to scream. Who knows how long I yelled? Suddenly, in the gathering dark, I heard a voice answer me, and I was filled with an inexpressible sense of liberation. In that tragic moment, I applied my fundamental human energy according to the purpose for which it was made, recovered my freedom to act, and moved my feet towards my salvation. That voice did not replace or eliminate me! It is terrible that in a case like this, humans often act as if they actually desperately preferred only to cry out, and refuse the possibility that a voice might bring help. And what Max Horkheimer affirms is true: "Without the revelation of a god, man can no longer manage to find a solution for himself."

In the *third place*, this hypothesis must respect *two conditions*, without which there would be no acceptable hypothesis at all:

a) If there really must be a revelation, as a word in addition to the one which the world already speaks to our unworthy hearts and inquiring intelligence, then it must be a word that is *comprehensible* to man. Therefore, in order for revelation, in its more restricted sense, to be such, to add something to the world's own enigmatic revelation, it must be translated into comprehensible terms. Otherwise it is like ultrasound, as if it did not exist.

b) Would not translating God into comprehensible terms be idolatry? Even if it is translated into human terms, the result of revelation must be the intensifying of mystery as mystery. It must not reduce mystery, like a human being saying, "I understand!" but rather deepen it. In this way, it is understood and yet always more understood as mystery. For example: the world and my own life depend on God. And this is true. But if we replace the enigmatic word "mystery" that reality suggests, with the word, "Father" that revelation implies, then we have an extremely comprehensible term, which is part of our experience: it is Father who gives me life, who has introduced me to the beauty of things, who has put me on my guard against possible dangers. Voilà: the Absolute, the Mystery, is Father, to repeat, "*tam pater nemo*." No one is such a Father. This truth that Christ has revealed does not diminish the Absolute. Rather, it deepens our knowledge of the mystery: Our Father who art at the depths, who art in heaven, Our Father who art in my profound roots, Thou who art now making me in this instant, who generate my path and guide me to my destiny! You can no longer retract after hearing these words of God. You can no longer go back. But, at the same time, the mystery remains, remains more profound: God is father, but he is father like no other is father. The revealed term carries the mystery further within you, closer to your flesh and bones, and you really feel it in a familiar way, as a son or daughter. There is no one who respects the sense of truth and is as devoted to his father as when the father is truly an intimate companion.

The fundamental dogma of the Enlightenment is the impossibility of a revelation. This is the taboo preached by all liberal philosophy and its materialistic heirs. The affirmation of this impossibility is the extreme attempt that reason makes in order to dictate by itself the measure of the real, and, therefore, the measure of the possible and impossible in reality. But the hypothesis of Revelation cannot be destroyed by any preconception or option. It raises a factual issue to which the nature of the human heart is originally open. This openness must prevail if life is to be realized. The destiny of the "religious sense" is totally tied to it.

This is the frontier of human dignity: "Even if salvation does not come, still I want to be worthy of it in every instant."[2]

Notes

CHAPTER ONE

1 Alexis Carrel, *Reflections on Life,* translated by Antonia White (London: Hamish Hamilton, 1952), 21, 23.
2 Ibid., 26.
3 St Augustine *Soliloquies* 1. 3. 8.
4 L. Giussani, *Il Rischio Educativo* (Turin: Società Editrice Internazionale, 1995), 53.
5 Aristotle *Topics* 1.11.105a3–7.
6 Dante *Inferno* 14.43–72.

CHAPTER TWO

1 The Council of Orange, can 5–8, in Denzinger-Schönmetzer, *Enchiridion Symbolorum,* nn. 375–8

CHAPTER THREE

1 Giacomo Leopardi, "To Sylvia," in *Selected Prose and Poetry,* translated by Iris Origo and John Heath-Stubbs (London: Oxford University Press 1966), 247.
2 Giuseppe Giusti, "Sant'Ambrogio," 15–16.
3 Fyodor Dostoyevsky, *The Devils,* translated by David Magarshack (Middlesex: Pensuin, 1971), 255.

CHAPTER FOUR

1 St Thomas Aquinas *Quaestiones disputatae de veritate* q.10. art.8c.
2 Jacques Leclercq, *Éloge de la paresse* (Brussels: Éditions de la cité chrétienne, 1937), 44.
3 G.K. Chesterton, *Orthodoxy* (London: John Lane, The Bodley Head, 1912), 51: "The modern world is full of the old Christian virtues gone mad."
4 J.W. von Goethe, *Faust,* translated by W.H. van der Smissen (London and Toronto: J.M. Dent & Sons Ltd., 1926), act 1, sc. 3 lines, 81–2.
5 *Summa Theologiae* 1. q.14. art.1.
6 Karl Jaspers, *Philosophical Faith and Revelation,* translated by E.B. Ashton (New York: Harper & Row, 1967), 97.

CHAPTER FIVE

1 Giacomo Leopardi, "Night Song of a Nomadic Shepherd in Asia," in *Selected Prose and Poetry,* translated by Iris Origo and John Heath-Stubbs (London: Oxford University Press, 1966), 275.
2 A.V. Arnault, "La feuille." "De la tige détachée/ pauvre feuille desséchée/ où vas-tu?" Leopardi translates this poem in his "Imitazione."
3 Rainer Maria Rilke, "The Second Elegy," in *Duino Elegies,* German text, with an English translation by J.B. Leishman and Stephen Spender (New York: W.W. Norton and Co., 1939), 31.
4 Eugenio Montale, *Cuttlefish Bones (1920–1927),* translated by William Arrowsmith (New York, London: W.W. Norton & Company, 1993), 119.
5 *The Poems of Leopardi,* translated by Geoffrey L. Bickersteth (Cambridge: Cambridge University Press, 1923), 285.
6 Giacomo Leopardi, *Pensieri* LXVIII, translated by W.S. Di Piero (Baton Rouge and London: Louisiana State University Press, 1981), 113.
7 Giacomo Leopardi, "On the Portrait of a Beautiful Lady," in *Selected Prose and Poetry,* translated by Iris Origo and John Heath-Stubbs (London: Oxford University Press, 1966), 285.
8 Rainer Maria Rilke, "Das Stundenbuch," *Poems from the Book of Hours,* translated by Babette Deutsch (New York: New Directions Publishing Corporation, 1941), 37.
9 Leopardi, "Night Song," in *Selected Prose,* 277–8.
10 Francesco Severi, "Itinerario di uno scienziato verso la fede," in *Dalla scienza alla fede* (Assisi: Edizioni Pro Civitate Christiana, 1959), 103. (*From Science to Faith.*)
11 "Scoppiò cinquant'anni fa la 'rivoluzione' di Einstein," *Corriere della Sera,* 20 April 1955, 3.
12 *Hamlet,* act 1, sc. 5, lines 166–7.

13 St Thomas Aquinas *Summa Theologiae* 1. q.20. art.1. Also see Dionysius *On the Divine Names* [59–63] cp 4.1c9.
14 Clemente Rebora, "Sandbags for the Eyes," lines 13–8.87–91.
15 Ugo Foscolo, "Dei sepolcri," lines 19–20.
16 Giacomo Leopardi, "Night Song," in *Selected Prose*, 277.
17 Fyodor Dostoyevsky, *The Devils*, translated by David Magarshack (Middlesex: Penguin Books, 1971), 54.
18 Ibid., 656.
19 Leopardi, *Selected Prose*, 215–16.
20 Cesare Pavese, *The Burning Brand: Diaries 1935–1950*, translated by A.E. Murch (New York: Walker & Company, 1961), 196.
21 Ibid., 345.
22 Ibid., 364, 283.
23 James Baldwin, *Blues for Mister Charlie* (New York: Dial Press, 1964), 19.
24 Thomas Mann, *Joseph and His Brothers*, translated from the German by H.T. Lowe-Porter (New York: Alfred A. Knopf, 1968), 3.
25 From Pavese's letter of 14 June 1949 to R. Calzecchi Onesti, in *Lettere 1926–1950* vol 2 (Turin: Einaudi, 1968), 655.
26 Alfred N. Whitehead, *Religion in the Making* (New York: Macmillan, 1927), 16.
27 Pär Lagerkvist, *Evening Land: Aftonland*, translated by W.H. Auden and Leif Sjöberg (Detroit: Wayne State University Press, 1975), 119.

CHAPTER SIX

1 Terence, *The Self-Tormentor*, edited by A.J. Brothers (Wiltshire: Aris & Phillips, 1988).
2 Natalino Sapegno, *Compendio di storia della letteratura italiana*, vol. 3 (Firenze: Nuova Italia, 1956), 240.
3 Eugenio Garin, *Cronache di filosofia italiana, 1900–1943* (Bari: Giuseppi Laterza et Figli, 1959), 529.
4 Dante *Paradiso* canto 22. v. 151.
5 John Dewey, *The Quest for Certainty* (London: George Allen & Unwin Ltd., 1930), 295.
6 Yevgeny Yevtushenko, "There are many who do not love me," in *Nuovi poeti sovetici*, edited by A.M. Ripellino (Turin: Einaudi, 1962), 163–4.
7 Bertrand Russell, "A Free Man's Worship," in *Mysticism and Logic and Other Essays* (London: George Allen & Unwin Ltd., 1951), 46–7.
8 Ibid., 47.
9 Kazimierz Brandys, "Obrona 'Grenady'" ("The Defense of Grenada"), in *Czerwona Czapeczka* (*The Little Red Hat*) (Warsaw: Panstwowy Institut Wydawniczy, 1957), 308.

10 R.L. Bensly, ed., "The Fourth Book of Ezra," in J.A. Robinson, ed., *Texts and Studies, Contributions to Biblical and Patristic Literature,* vol. 3, pt. 3 (Cambridge: Cambridge University Press, 1893).
11 Yevgeny Yevtushenko, "In Overcrowded Trams," in *Poesie,* translated from the Italian (Milan: Garzanti, 1970), 91–2.
12 Ernest Hemingway, *A Farewell to Arms* (New York: Macmillan, 1957), 331–2.

> Outside the room in the hall, I spoke to the doctor, "Is there anything I can do to-night?"
> "No. There is nothing to do. Can I take you to your hotel?"
> "No, thank you. I am going to stay here a while."
> "I know there is nothing to say. I cannot tell you –"
> "No," I said. "There's nothing to say."
> "Good-night," he said. "I cannot take you to your hotel?"
> "No, thank you."
> "It was the only thing to do," he said. "The operation proved –"
> "I do not want to talk about it," I said.
> "I would like to take you to your hotel."
> "No, thank you."
> He went down the hall. I went to the door of the room.
> "You can't come in now," one of the nurses said.
> "Yes I can," I said.
> "You can't come in yet."
> "You get out," I said. "The other one too."
> But after I had got them out and shut the door and turned off the light it wasn't any good. It was like saying good-by to a statue. After a while I went out and left the hospital and walked back to the hotel in the rain.

13 Thomas Mann, "Little Herr Friedmann," in *Children and Fools,* translated by George Schaffauer (New York: Alfred A. Knopf, 1928).
14 Giosuè Carducci, *Poems,* translated by Maud Holland (London: T. Fisher Unwin, 1907), 94:

> Alas! and alas! the train fled onward rushing
>   While I was weeping thus within my heart,
> And a merry company of young colts came pushing,
>   Neighing and jostling, to see the wonder start.
>
> But a silvery donkey on a thistle grazing,
>   A thorny, purple thistle, scarce listened to their tread,
> He heeded not the clamour, nor all the stir amazing,
>   But thoughtfully and slowly bit off the thistle's head.

A.J. Cronin, *The Stars Look Down* (Boston: Little, Brown & Company, 1935); "Il libro," in *Primi poemetti,* vv. 10–13.

CHAPTER SEVEN

1 Nikos Kazantzakis, *The Odyssey,* translated by Kimon Friar (New York: Simon and Schuster, 1958), 2.
2 *A Selection from the Poems of Giosuè Carducci,* translated by Emily A. Tribe (London: Longmans, Green and Co., 1921), 127.
3 See André Gide, *If it Die,* translated by Dorothy Bussy (London: Secker & Warburg, 1955), 258ff.
4 Yevgeny Yevtushenko, "After Every Lesson," in *Poesie,* translated from the Italian (Milan: Garzanti, 1970), 40–1.
5 See T. Adorno, *Minima Moralia: Reflections from Damaged Life,* translated by E.F.N. Jephcott (London: Bookcraft Ltd., 1989), 105–6.
6 Pavese, *The Burning Brand: Diaries 1935–1950,* translated by A.E. Murch (New York: Walker & Company, 1961), 283.
7 Jack Kerouac, *Visions of Cody* (New York: McGraw-Hill Book Company, 1972), 91–2.
8 Giacomo Leopardi, *Selected Prose and Poetry,* translated by Iris Origo and John Heath-Stubbs (London: Oxford University Press, 1966), 283.
9 Eugenio Montale, "Perhaps Some Morning ...," in *Provisional Conclusions,* translated by Edith Farnsworth (Chicago: Henry Regnery Co., 1970), 40.
10 Cesare Pavese, "Earth and Death," *A Mania for Solitude: Selected Poems 1930–1950,* translated by Margaret Crosland (London: Peter Owen, 1969), 123.
11 Fyodor Dostoyevsky, *The Brothers Karamazov,* translated by David Magarshack (Middlesex: Penguin Books, 1974), 285.
12 Paul Claudel, *The Tidings Brought to Mary: A Mystery,* translated by Louise Morgan Sill (New Haven, Connecticut: Yale University Press, 1916), 157–8.
13 Denis Diderot, *Oeuvres,* edited by J. Assézat and M. Tourneux (Paris, 1875–9), 18:101.
14 Andrei Voznesensky, "Oza," *Antiworlds and the Fifth Race,* translated by William J. Smith/Max Hayward (New York: Basic Books, 1967), 239–41.
15 From Winston Churchill's address at MIT on 31 March 1949; quoted in John Ely Burchard, ed., *Mid-Century: the Social Implications of Scientific Progress* (New York: MIT Press, 1950).
16 "... every blade of grass, every small insect, and, golden bee, all of them knew so marvellously their path, and without possessing the faculty of reason, bore witness to the mystery of God, constantly partaking in it themselves." Fyodor Dostoyevsky, *The Broths Karamazov,* translated by David Magarshak (Middlesex: Penguin Books, 1971), 346.

CHAPTER EIGHT

1 Han Yü (768–824), *Fragments of Chinese Doctrine.*
2 Anonymous writer, quoted in *Samizdat: cronaca di una vita nuova nell'urss* (Milan: Russia Cristiana, 1975), 156.
3 Alexander I. Solzhenitsyn, *The Nobel Lecture on Literature,* translated by Thomas P. Whitney (New York: Harper & Row, 1971), 21.
4 Dante *Inferno* 8. v. 19.
5 Pierre Teilhard de Chardin, *The Phenomenon of Man* (New York: Harper & Brothers Publishers, 1959), 230–1
6 Cesare Pavese, *Il compagno* (Turin: Einaudi, 1950).
7 Sergei Chudakov, "Man overboard!," in *Testi letterari e poesie: Da riviste clandestine dell'URSS,* translated from the Italian (Milan: Jaca Book, 1966), 43.
8 Artemi Michajlov, in ibid., 117.
9 See, among others, St Augustine, *The City of God* xix. 3. 3.
10 *Romeo and Juliet,* act 2, sc. 2, lines 47–9: "Romeo, doff thy name; And for thy name, which is no part of thee, Take all myself."
11 See Gaius, *Institutionum Comentarii Quattuor,* II. 12–17 and Marcus Terentius Varro, *Rerum Rusticarum Libri Tres* 1. 17.
12 See Anton Makarenko, *Problems of Soviet School Education* (Moscow: Progress Publishers, 1965), 32, 137–8.
13 Czeslaw Milosz, *Selected Poems* (New York: The Seabury Press, 1973), 109.
14 Pius X, *Catechism of Christian Doctrine,* I. III. 53.
15 Boris Pasternak, *Doctor Zhivago,* translated by Max Hayward and Manya Harari (London: Collins and Harvill Press, 1958), 268.
16 Aleksander I. Solzhenitsyn, *The Gulag Archipelago,* translated by Thomas P. Whitney (New York: Harper & Row, 1973), 173–4.
17 Maxim Gorky, *Lenin* (Rome: Editori Riuniti, 1975), 67–8.
18 Rabindranath Tagore, *Gitanajali* ("Song Offerings"), translated by Tagore (London: Macmillan, 1913), 25–6.

CHAPTER NINE

1 Barbara Ward, *Faith and Freedom* (Garden City, NY: Image Books, 1958), 14.
2 Cesare Pavese, *Lettere 1924–44* (Turin: Einaudi, 1966), 7.
3 Plato, *Gorgias,* translated by Robin Waterfield (Oxford: Oxford University Press, 1994), 114.
4 Pierre Lecomte du Noüy, *L'avenir de l'esprit* (Paris: Gallimard, 1941).
5 Aleksander I. Solzhenitsyn, *Cancer Ward,* translated by Nicholas Bethell and David Burg (New York: Bantam Books, 1969), 435–6.
6 Andrey Sinyavsky, *Unguarded Thoughts,* translated by Manya Harari (London: Collins & Harvill Press, 1972), 65.

7 Ludwig Wittgenstein, *Tractatus Logico-Philosophicus,* translated by D.F. Pearse and B.F. McGuiness (Atlantic Highland, NJ: Humanities Press International, 1992).

8 Immanuel Kant, *Critique of Pure Reason,* translated by Norman Kemp Smith (London: Macmillan, 1934), 5.

CHAPTER TEN

1 Abraham Joshua Heschel, *God in Search of Man* (New York: Farrar, Straus & Giroux, 1955), 251, 253.

2 Alberto Caracciolo, *La religione come struttura e come modo autonomo della conoscenza* (Milan: Marietti, 1965), 24.

3 Job 38.

4 Immanuel Kant, *Critique of Practical Reason,* translated by Thomas Kingsmill Abbott, 5th ed. (London: Longmans, Green & Co., 1898), 260.

5 Wisd. 13:1–15.

6 Gen. 8:21ff.

7 Acts 14:15–17.

8 Giovanni Pascoli, "La voce," in *Canti di Castelvecchio.*

9 *The Antigone of Sophocles,* an English version by Dudley Fitts and Robert Fitzgerald (London: Humphrey Milford, 1938), 32.

CHAPTER ELEVEN

1 Clemente Rebora, "From the Taut Image," in *Canti anonimi,* translated from the Italian.

2 St Augustine *Commentary on the Gospel of St John* 26.5.

3 Plato, *Symposium* XXIX. 211b–212b.

4 Francesco Severi, "Itinerario di uno scienziato verso la fede," in *Dalla scienza alla fede* (Assisi: Edizioni Pro Civitate Christiana, 1959), 103.

5 Act 1, sc. 1, lines 237–9.

6 "Il Pioppo," in *Canti dell'infermità.* Translated from the Italian.

7 See Gabriel Marcel, *The Mystery of Being* I (Chicago: Henry Regnery Company, 1960), 261ff.

8 *The Germania of Tacitus,* with English notes by Alfred J. Church (London: Macmillan, 1886), 144–5.

9 Fyodor Dostoyevsky, *The Devils,* translated by David Magarshack (Middlesex: Penguin Books, 1971), 233: "If there is no God, then what sort of captain am I after that."

CHAPTER TWELVE

1 *The Comedy of Dante Alighieri,* Purgatory, translated by Dorothy L. Sayers (Middlesex: Penguin Books, 1955), 17:127–9.

2 Clemente Rebora, *Canti anonimi,* translated by Margherita Marchione (Boston: Twayne Publishers 1979), 102, 104.
3 *Macbeth,* act 5, sc. 5, line 26.
4 Albert Einstein, *The World as I See It* (New York: Covici-Friede, 1934), 242, 237.

CHAPTER THIRTEEN

1 Graham Greene, *The End of the Affair* (London: Penguin Books, 1975), 175–6. The actual conversation is as follows:
  Bendrix: "Your church certainly goes in for superstition in a big way – St Januarius, bleeding statues, visions of the virgin – that sort of thing."
  Father Crompton: "We try to sort them out. And isn't it more sensible to believe that anything may happen?"
2 Cardinal John Henry Newman, *Apologia pro vita sua* (Boston: Houghton Mifflin Company, 1956), 24–5.
3 Gilbert K. Chesterton, *The Man Who Was Thursday* (Middlesex: Penguin Books, 1988), 88.

CHAPTER FOURTEEN

1 *Inferno* 26.85–142.
2 Acts 17:24–8.
3 Ugo Foscolo, "Dei sepolcri" (Bergamo: Cinque Vie, 1985), lines 19–10.
4 Rom. 1:22–31.
5 T.S. Eliot, "Choruses from 'The Rock' VI," in *Collected Poems 1909–1935* (London: Faber and Faber, 1936), 170–1.
6 St Thomas Aquinas, *Summa Theologiae* I. q.1. art.1.
7 Plato *Phaedo,* translated by G.M.A. Grube (Indianapolis: Hackett Publishing Co., 1977), 36.

CHAPTER FIFTEEN

1 T.S. Eliot, "The Four Quartets," in *Collected Poems 1909–1962* (New York: Harcourt, Brace & World, Inc. 1963), 198.
2 See Gustav Janouch, *Conversations with Kafka,* translated by Goronwy Rees (London: Quartet Books, 1985), 166. "I try to be a true attendant upon grace. Perhaps it will come – perhaps it will not come. Perhaps this quiet yet unquiet waiting is the harbinger of grace or perhaps it is grace itself. I do not know. But that does not disturb me."

Subject Index

Author Index

Permissions